HAPPY FEET

HOW TO BE A
GOLD STAR SOCCER PARENT

(Everything the Coach, the Ref and

Your Kid Want You to Know)

BY DAN BLANK

ISBN: 0989697703
ISBN 13: 9780989697705
Soccer Poet LLC

INTRODUCTION

Congratulations! You've got yourself a soccer playing child! Maybe you've got more than one of them. Even better! You are among the millions of soccer parents who will spend countless weekends in the great outdoors under sunny skies, making friends and memories and sharing an incredible experience that your child will cherish long after his or her playing career is finished.

There will be thrilling victories and agonizing defeats and heroic performances. There will be amazing goals and acrobatic saves and edge-of-your-seat suspense. And best of all, there will form an irreplaceable camaraderie among the players and parents that share in this experience. It's going to be the journey of a lifetime!

Awesome, right!

At least that is how it's supposed to work. And if you play your role properly, that's exactly how it will work. You'll be headed for a life of soccer bliss, just the way the world has intended. But stay alert! This road you'll travel is filled with many deep and dangerous potholes. If you don't navigate them with vigilance, your voyage will end prematurely, as it has for so many others.

Did you know that in the United States, 75% of children that play youth sports quit by the age of 13? Do you know why? Well, I'm sure you can guess, but I'll tell you anyway. The number one reason children give for quitting a sport is this: It stopped being fun.

Do you know the number one reason why sports stop being fun? Yep, you guessed it again: Adults. Parental behaviors are a major contributor to the mortality rate of youth sports participation. In the world of youth sports, well-intentioned parents have a remarkable knack for unwittingly devolving into joyless fun-suckers who drive their children away from the sports they once loved. Hard to believe, right?

Soccer drop-out rates fall right in line with national averages. 75% of our kids drop out of soccer because the fun gets sucked out of it, often by parents. That should frighten the heck out of you. Can you imagine if three out of every four students dropped out of high school? If our high school dropout rate was 75%, our country would be scrambling day and night to find a solution; it would be the preeminent issue of every presidential election campaign; it would be a national emergency – the problem we couldn't go without solving. But because it is just a matter of kids playing sports, an issue that only concerns the vast majority of parents until their children finish high school, we are content to let it pass until it's the next guy's problem.

But remember this: sports are awesome! Soccer is awesome! Especially when you are a kid! Youth soccer is a big, big deal when you are a youth soccer player. When the bedroom lights go out, a child lays in bed replaying the game he just won or the goal he just scored or the goal he'll score tomorrow. Some kids are so excited for tomorrow's match that they go to bed in their uniforms. Others sleep curled up next to a soccer ball. And throughout the night they dream great, big, wonderful soccer dreams. How can a kid who loves the game this much be pried away from it? Well, there is a list of ways, and at the top of that list are Mom and Dad.

This book isn't a collection of sideline horror stories. It isn't for the knuckleheads who make national headlines every few months for inciting a riot on the sidelines. Those folks constitute a miniscule fraction of the sideline population, and no book I could ever write will help them to rehabilitate. This book is for all those soccer parents who start the soccer journey with their hearts in the right place and the very best of intentions. I'm talking about you.

Somehow, despite their noble motives, emotionally stable and well-meaning parents from coast to coast end up with a child who has lost his love for the sport and decides to walk away from it. Too often the best of intentions leads to the worst possible outcome. Let's face it; no parent starts out this journey with the idea of eventually persuading his child to quit. But with a 75% drop-out rate, you can't logically assume that this is something that only happens to the other guy. And moms, just because I used the expression *other guy*, don't feel that you are absolved from this discussion. You're just as guilty as the dads. You'll realize that before you finish this book. But fret not! I'm going to help you. I'm going to be your navigator and your early-warning radar. I'm going to light your path so you don't inadvertently wind up as an unsuspecting fun-sucker.

My goal for this book is that by the end, you, the reader, will be able to avoid the potholes that can turn your soccer player into a statistic. It doesn't matter if your child is seven or seventeen. It doesn't matter if he plays rec soccer or college soccer. It doesn't matter if you are a seasoned veteran of the travel soccer grind or you are completely new to the sport, there are things in these pages that you need to know. There are things in here that will help you. I promise.

Because soccer has so many sub-segments in terms of gender, age, and competitive level (rec, school, club), it's often impossible to issue a blanket statement that applies to every player at every age or competitive level. Not all of these ideas will be applicable to every single demographic, but most of them will. I'll leave it up to you to differentiate between the concepts that don't apply to your child and those that do.

This is an equal opportunity book. I don't care if you played in a World Cup or never even kicked a soccer ball; I will give you a working vocabulary about a game you might know almost nothing about, and I will disseminate the information that your coach, your referee and most importantly, your child want you to know about being a soccer parent. I will give you the Do's and Don'ts of being an extraordinary soccer parent; a parent who allows your soccer player to experience all of the joy that soccer can and should bring into his life. Remember, soccer, above all else, should be fun. It should be fun for your children and it should be fun for you. If you pay attention to what you are about to read, you'll stand a much better chance of keeping it that way.

Are you ready to begin this journey? I hope you are! I've recruited coaches from New Jersey to California to help me give you the best possible guidance. I hope you are ready and excited and bursting at the seams with anticipation! I hope you're thinking that you are going to be the best darn soccer parent of all time! Because if that's what you're thinking... well then, you've just chosen your destination. And we never start a journey without first knowing where we want to end up. I hope you will choose a destination that is worthy of you and your child. I want soccer to be something your whole family enjoys for many years, so stay with me on this journey. By the end, you will be a Gold Star Soccer Parent empowered to help your child enjoy many years with a pair of very Happy Feet!

TABLE OF CONTENTS

SECTION 1
SOCCERSPEAK

1

A Working Vocabulary

You don't need to know a darn thing about soccer to be a Gold Star Soccer Parent, but if soccer is going to be part of your family's life, then you may want to have a working vocabulary of its terms. That's what I'm about to give you. If you already have a strong soccer background or don't give a hoot about soccer's terminology, don't sweat it. Just skip ahead to SECTION 2. I'll catch up to you there.

If you're still hanging around, I appreciate your resolve. You crave a broader understanding of this strange game your child plays each weekend. There's something noble about that.

Please keep in mind that many structural elements of soccer change to accommodate the age range of the players. For the younger age groups, the size of the field, the size of the goals, the size of the ball, the number of players and even the number of officials are all smaller than what you'll find at the high school, college and professional level. Unless otherwise noted, the terms in this section refer to full-sided, 11v11 soccer.

If you're a true newbie to soccer, then some of this might seem like a foreign language. I'm going to do my best to keep the explanations simple and conversational. I've also created SoccerPepper™ companion videos to provide a visual explanation of certain terms. I highly recommend that you take advantage of these videos. You can access these videos online at www.youtube.com/user/HappyFeetBook.

As a jumping off point, I'm going to assume you know that a soccer team is comprised of ten field players and one goalkeeper, and that the goalkeeper is the one who is dressed differently than everyone else and is allowed to use his hands. I'm assuming you know what a sideline is and what an end-line is and that if Team A knocks the ball out of bounds, possession is awarded to Team B. And I am assuming you know that the object of the game is to put the ball into your opponent's goal more times than the opponent puts the ball into yours. Those are the very basics. But since at some point or another you may want to talk about soccer without making your child cringe in embarrassment, let's get into some semi-advanced terminology that you'll want to know. This won't earn you your soccer Ph.D., but it'll get you moving in the right direction.

THE FIELD

Center Circle – The circle in the center of the field. Its diameter is 20 yards.

'D' – The *'D'* is the arc at the top of the 18. Any point along that arc is ten yards from the penalty spot.

Eighteen (18) – Also known as the *18-yard box*, the *penalty area*, the *penalty box* or just *the box*. This is the big rectangle in front of each goal that extends 18 yards wide of each post and 18 yards forward from the endline. This is the area where the goalkeeper is allowed to use his hands to handle the ball. When a direct free kick is whistled against the defending team in this area, the attacking team is awarded a penalty kick.

Six (6) – Also known as the *'goal box.'* The six-yard box is the smaller rectangle in front of each goal. It extends six yards wide of each post and six yards forward off the endline. The primary function of this box is to dictate where goal kicks are taken.

Take a look at the brief SoccerPepper™ Lesson 1 video entitled *The Field*. All of these terms are explained in the video, so you'll be off to a running start!

OFFICIALS – MEET YOUR REFEREES.

A.R. – That's the assistant referee, formerly known as the linesman, and his job is to assist the referee. These are the guys who carry the flags but no whistles. The A.R.'s primary responsibilities are alerting the center official when the ball goes out of bounds and when there has been an infraction of the offside rule. The A.R. is also responsible for monitoring substitutions.

Center Official – The referee. He's the one in charge so he carries the whistle.

RULES and RESTARTS – Let's clarify a few of these for you.

Advantage – The center official's prerogative to ignore a foul when he feels that calling the foul would be detrimental to the team that was fouled. More about this later.

Free Kick – Free kicks are awarded after a foul has been called and also for restarting play when the ball has gone out of bounds over the goal line. The tap-offs to start a half and after a goal has been scored can also be considered free kicks. Free kicks are divided into two categories: indirect and direct. The nature of the infraction determines whether a kick is indirect or direct.

Indirect Free Kick – A restart, after a foul has been called, that requires two players to touch the ball before it can enter the goal. That second player can be from either team. The referee will signal an indirect free kick by keeping his arm raised until a second player has touched the ball. The most common infractions resulting in indirect free kicks are offside, obstruction and dangerous play.

Direct Free Kick – A restart, after a foul has been called, that allows the attacking team to score directly from the ensuing kick without the ball having to touch a second player. Corner kicks and tap-offs are also direct free kicks. The most common infractions resulting in direct free kicks are tripping, pushing and hand balls.

Goal Kick – A direct free kick restart for the defending team when a player from the attacking team is the last person to touch the ball before it goes out-of-bounds across the end-line.

Corner Kick – A direct free kick restart for the attacking team when a player from the defending team is the last person to touch the ball before it goes out-of-bounds across the end-line.

Goal – The result of the entire ball crossing the entire goal-line within the frame of the goal.

Hand Ball – Illegal use of the hand or arm to affect the ball that results in a direct free kick.

Half-time – An intermission after the first half of play. The teams switch ends of the field for the second half.

In-Bounds / Out-of-Bounds – The ball is considered in-bounds until the entire ball crosses over the entire end-line or sideline. Unlike basketball, a soccer ball does not have to touch the ground to be ruled out-of-bounds. As soon as the entire ball is over the entire line, it is considered to be out-of-bounds, even if it bends back onto the field of play.

Offside – We'll explain offside in more detail a little bit later. For now let's just say it is a rule put in place to prevent players from cherry-picking.

Penalty Kick – A direct free kick awarded to the attacking team when an opposing player has committed a foul inside his team's own penalty area.

Penalty Spot – The spot from where a penalty kick is taken. It is 12 yards from the center of the goal-line.

Yellow Card – A formal warning issued from the referee as a result of dangerous, unsportsmanlike or persistent behavior beyond the rules of the game. If a player or coach receives a second yellow card during the same match, he is ejected from the contest. In other words, two yellow cards equal one red card.

Red Card – A card issued by the referee to signal that a player or coach has been ejected from a contest. When a player is ejected from a game, he cannot be replaced. If a player from Team A is ejected, then Team A will be playing with 10 players while Team B will still use 11 players.

Stoppage Time – The amount of time a referee can choose to add onto the end of a half based on the stoppages that occurred during that half for things like injuries, goals and yellow cards. This discretion given to the referee does not exist at many youth levels.

Ten Yards – The minimum distance the defending team must remain from the ball prior to the opponent taking a free kick.

Throw-In – A throw-in is a restart employed when the ball goes out-of-bounds over a sideline. If a player on Team A is the last person to touch the ball before it goes over the sideline, a throw-in is awarded to Team B.

Wall – A line of players positioned between an opponent's free kick and the goal. They form a human wall intended to block out a portion of the goal. You'll often see a referee march off ten yards to indicate where the wall may position itself. (See Ten Yards above.)

Take a look at SoccerPepper™ Lesson 2 video entitled *Rules and Restarts*.

VERNACULAR

Just like NASCAR, tennis and poker, soccer has a language of its own. Use this guide to help translate what your kid just said.

Bar – Short for crossbar.

Bender – A bender refers to a ball that follows a curved path. Yes, players can make the ball curve when they kick it. Think *'Bend it Like Beckham.'*

Boots – Soccer shoes.

Brace – Two goals by a single player in a single game.

Chip – A chip is a soft, flighted ball, normally with backspin.

Combination – A brief series of attacking passes and movements designed to eliminate defenders. You'll learn more about these later.

Crossbar – The top, horizontal piece of a goal that connects the two vertical posts. Also known as *the bar*.

Dummy – A dummy is a maneuver where a player deliberately lets the ball roll through her legs with the intention of it arriving to a teammate who is behind her.

Equalizer – A goal that ties the score.

Football – A synonym for soccer. Also referred to as *footie*.

Goal-Side – The space between an opponent (or the ball) and the goal you are defending. You may hear a coach say something like: "*When defending, it is important to get goal-side of your opponent.*"

Hat Trick – Three goals by a single player in a single game.

High / Low – These terms refer to a direction or area on the field. '*High*' means closer to the opponent's goal while '*low*' means closer to your own goal.

Instep – The top of your foot. Also known as the *laces* or *shoelaces*.

Juggling – Keeping a soccer ball off the ground without using your arms or hands.

Kit – The uniform. For tomorrow's match we'll be wearing our all-red kit.

Mark or Marking – Soccer's equivalent of guarding a player in basketball. It's the defensive responsibility of shadowing an opponent and trying to shut him down. The coach might say, "*Today Alex is going to mark their #7. Alex, don't let that #7 even touch the ball.*"

Meg – Short for nutmeg.

Negative Ball – A backward pass.

Nutmeg – Maneuvering the ball through an opponent's legs.

Pitch – A synonym for soccer field.

Play On! – A verbal directive from the center official to alert the players that he will not be blowing his whistle (because he has either judged a questionable play to be legal or he plans to apply the advantage rule) and that they should continue playing.

Shield – To protect the ball from an opponent by positioning your body between the opponent and the ball.

Square – As in *square pass* or *square ball*; a lateral pass; a pass that runs parallel to the end-line.

Surface – A body part used to receive or play the ball such as the chest, head, outside of the foot, etc.

Switch – To move the ball laterally from one side of the field to the other. Also referred to as *switching fields* or *switching the point of attack*.

System – The formation of defenders, midfielders and forwards a team deploys such as a 4-4-2 or 4-3-3. You'll learn more about this later.

Tackle – The act of physically separating an opponent from the ball.

Third – In soccer we often refer to the field in thirds: the defensive third, the middle third and the attacking third.

Trap – The skill of receiving and settling/stopping a moving ball.

Upper 90 – The top corner on either side of the goal where the post and cross-bar form a 90-degree angle.

Volley – The act of kicking a ball that is in midair. Variations include the half-volley and the side-volley.

2

The Positions
And Roles

One of the great things about soccer is that it is not a very position-specific sport. In football, for example, the lineman's job is very different from the quarterback's whose job is very different from the wide receiver whose job is very different from the linebacker whose job is very different from the punter's. Each of those players possesses a distinct skill set.

In soccer, with the exception of the goalkeeper, the players have very similar skill sets regardless of their respective positions. Everyone needs to be able to receive, dribble, pass and shoot a ball. Additionally, in soccer, any player can go anywhere on the field at any given time. Yes, it's rare to see a goalkeeper run into the attacking half of the field, but it is very common for a defender to end up close to the opponent's goal, or for a forward to find himself defending inside his team's penalty box. I'm sure this might seem a little chaotic, but stick with me and you'll get the hang of it.

Generally speaking, here are the positions and roles of the players on the field. Again I am referring to full-sided, 11v11 soccer.

Goalkeeper – The goalkeeper is the one who is dressed differently than the rest of her teammates. She is allowed to handle the ball anywhere inside of her own penalty area. The goalkeeper's primary responsibility is to prevent the ball from entering her team's goal.

Defenders – Defenders play in front of the goalkeeper but behind the midfielders. Most teams use four defenders. The primary job of the defenders is to keep the opponent from scoring.

Midfielders – Midfielders play in front of the defenders but behind the forwards. They typically do the most running as they are responsible for attacking and defending. As a loose rule of thumb, midfielders are expected to play from '18 to 18.' When a team is in possession of the ball, the central midfielders serve as a link between the defenders and the forwards, and from the right side to the left.

Forwards – The forwards play in front of the midfielders. Their primary responsibility is to score goals, but they also share in some of the defending responsibilities. They are also expected to hold the ball under pressure when their team is advancing out of its defensive end.

Take a look at the SoccerPepper™ Lesson 3 video entitled *Positions*.

3

The Four Pillars

Soccer players are judged by four main criteria: technical, tactical, physical and psychological. We refer to these as the Four Pillars.

Technical – This simply refers to what a player can do with the ball. It's another word for talent. The more talented a player is on the ball, the more technical she is said to be.

Tactical – Tactics are the decisions a soccer player is faced with at any and all points of the game, regardless of who has the ball. The tactical pillar is your soccer brain. A player with an advanced tactical sense is said to have a high soccer IQ.

Physical – As you might expect, the physical pillar refers to a player's physical tools such as size, speed, strength, agility and leaping ability.

Psychological – The psychological pillar refers to such things as a player's competitiveness, mental toughness, work rate, dependability, and effect on team chemistry.

In the scheme of player development, the technical pillar is the foundation for everything else. It doesn't matter how fast, tough or smart you are if you can't kick or trap a ball.

4

What The Heck Is Offside?

Soccer is governed by 17 Laws of the Game. These laws are sometimes tweaked by various organizations to accommodate the different needs of the participants. For example, the field size and number of players is different for 5-year-olds than it is for professionals. Still, the 17 Laws of the Game provide the framework for what is and is not acceptable conduct on the soccer field. In short, they are the rules.

By now you are probably familiar with the more common infractions. You know that a player other than the goalkeeper cannot handle the ball in the field of play, and that a player may not trip an opponent. These are pretty self-explanatory. The rules that cause the most problems at all levels of soccer are offside and advantage. I'll do my best to explain them for you.

As stated in Law 11:

A player is in an offside position if he/she is nearer to his/her opponents' goal line than both the ball and the second to last opponent. (In almost all cases the opposition goalkeeper will be one of the two opponents keeping a player on-side.)

Note: A player is not in an offside position if:

- *He is in his own half of the field of play*
- *He is level with the second to last opponent*
- *He is level with the last two opponents*

Offside Offense/Violation - A player in an offside position is only penalized if, at the moment the ball touches or is played by one of his team, he is, in the opinion of the referee, involved in active play by:

- *Interfering with play*
- *Interfering with an opponent*
- *Gaining an advantage by being in that position*

No Offside Offense/Violation - The off-side law is not applicable when a player receives the ball from:

- *A goal kick*
- *A throw-in*
- *A corner kick*

If a player is deemed to be offside by the referee, the opposing team is awarded an indirect free kick from the place where the violation occurred.

Simple, right? Is it any wonder this is the most misunderstood rule in soccer?

It may help if you understand the point of even having a rule that is so complex. The offside rule exists to prevent a team from leaving a player or players up near the opponent's goal looking for chances to score easy goals. It may help if you think of a basketball team that leaves one player under the opponent's basket even when the opponent has the ball. This is referred to as cherry-picking. The offside rule forces teams to work the ball up the field as a unit, as opposed to just bombing the ball forward to a cherry-picker. It keeps the 20 field players more tightly grouped, ensuring that defensive pressure can be more readily applied to the ball-carrier, which keeps the game moving faster. If it wasn't for the offside rule, soccer would look a whole lot different. Instead of 20 field players grouped in a segment of the field, you'd have a large pack of players near one goal, a large pack of players near the other, and a few midfielders trying to move the ball from one of these packs to the other. It would take away a great deal of soccer's aesthetic beauty of passing and possession and turn it into a game of boom ball. So in summary, the offside rule prevents cherry-picking. Make sense?

When it comes to deciding whether or not a play is offside, you must remember it has nothing to do with where the attacker was when he received the ball, but where he was in the instant the ball was played. If he was even with, or in front of the deepest defender, or on his own half of the field, there is no offside violation. The most difficult part for the official is determining where the attacker was at the precise moment that the ball was played. Forwards regularly stand even with the deepest defender, and often times the pass in question was played from 30 yards or further down the field. It can be very difficult for the A.R. to see all the pieces of this puzzle in a single field of vision, which is why offside is the most disputed call in our game.

As you can tell from reading Law 11, there are many parameters for an offside occurrence, but the most common one occurs when a forward on Team A is deeper than the entire line of defenders on Team B when the ball is played in behind Team B's defense. If you can understand that, you're halfway home. And please, make sure you remember that a player cannot be offside in his own defensive half of the field.

The SoccerPepper™ Lesson 4 video entitled *Offside* provides a visual representation of the offside rule and its nuances.

5

Advantage

Are you familiar with the NFL? If you are, you know that when one team is flagged for a penalty, the other team has the option of declining that penalty. The advantage rule is very similar, except it is the referee who decides, during the run of play, if a team that was fouled is better served by not having that foul called. For example...

A midfielder sends a beautiful pass in behind the opponent's defense and her teammate who receives that pass is going to have an excellent chance to score. However, just as the midfielder released her pass, she was fouled by an opponent. The referee has a choice to make: either call the foul and award a free kick, or invoke the advantage rule and see how things play out. The referee may decide that calling the foul would actually do more harm to the attacking team (negating their ADVANTAGE) and apply the advantage rule.

The point of the advantage rule is to not reward a team for fouling an opponent and to avoid punishing a team that has been fouled. This is often an exceptionally difficult call, even for the very best referees, because they have to evaluate the circumstances very quickly and reach a decision.

Referees are granted a little leeway should they decide to invoke advantage. For starters, if it quickly becomes clear that no advantage would materialize, the referee may change his mind, whistle the foul and award the free kick.

If the referee deems that the foul was worthy of a yellow or red card (caution or ejection), he can still elect to apply the advantage and then at the next stoppage, caution or eject the player who committed the foul.

The advantage rule, although absolutely stellar in theory, is much more difficult when it comes to practical application. Referees must make a snap judgment while everything around them is moving at breakneck speed. But when you're on the sideline and you're certain that you just saw a foul that went unwhistled, see if the ref is waving play on and shouting, *"Advantage!"* If he is, you'll know what he's talking about.

To see the advantage rule being applied, check out the SoccerPepper™ Lesson 5 video entitled *Advantage*.

6

The Hand Ball

I've been playing soccer since 1975 and coaching it since 1991 and the only thing I'm sure of is that no one, including the officials, is absolutely certain of what constitutes a hand ball. There are as many interpretations as there are referees and coaches and players.

According to Law 12, a hand ball is a violation when a player handles the ball *deliberately*. Okay, that's easy enough. The problem is that a very small percentage of hand balls are actually deliberate and there is at least one built in contradiction. A player who is guilty of an intentional hand ball is given a yellow card. Well then, by definition, every hand ball should be a yellow card, right? Except that's not the case.

Also, if the letter of the law actually carried the day, you wouldn't see professional soccer players keeping their hands behind their backs when they are inside of their own penalty areas trying to block shots or crosses. If an attacker fires a shot and it hits a defender in the arm, that's hardly deliberate, but it's often whistled as a penalty kick. Like I said, I'm pretty sure no one knows exactly what qualifies as a hand ball.

So here are my unofficial criteria for a hand ball:

- *Any part of the hand and arm can be involved.*
- *If it significantly affects the path of the ball, particularly if it benefits the team that handled the ball, it's a hand ball.*
- *The higher the hand is raised, the more likely a hand ball will be called.*
- *The farther the arm is extended away from the body, the more likely a handball will be called.*

Unofficially, that's how most officials decide whether or not to whistle a hand ball and most coaches would consider that definition reasonable. You will notice that there can be a great variation from one referee to the next when it comes to hand balls. You're just going to have to get used to it.

7

Systems

The terms 'system' and 'style' are often confused, but they are certainly not interchangeable. We'll talk about styles in the next chapter.

System simply refers to the formation of field players. When verbalizing a team's system, you always start with the number of defenders, then midfielders, then forwards. For example, a team that plays with three defenders, five midfielders and two forwards is said to be playing a 3-5-2.

Each digit represents a line of positions. The sum of the digits in a system should always add up to ten: 3+5+2 = 10. (It goes without saying that each team will play with one goalkeeper, so we do not factor the goalkeeper into the verbalization of systems. That is why systems add up to ten even though there are 11 players on the field.)

Other common soccer systems are:

4-4-2

4-5-1

4-3-3

3-4-3

Although the digits always add up to ten, there can be more than three digits. For example, over the past several years, the 4-2-3-1 has become very popular. There is an added line of midfielders in this formation.

There can also be fewer than three lines of players. For example, Spain has done very well in deploying a 4-6-0.

Regardless, we always start with the number of defenders and work our way forward. And the numbers always add up to ten. There are no rules governing a team's system. The players can be deployed in any manner the coach chooses. I've shared the most common systems with you, but there would be nothing illegal about a team playing in a 1-1-8. As long as the numbers add up to ten, the deployment is perfectly legal.

It is important to note that a team can change its system from one game to the next, or even multiple times within the same game. It just depends on how the coach decides to deploy his players. A common change in system occurs when a team is trailing late in the game and needs to score a goal. A team that has played in a 4-4-2 from the start of the game may elect to switch to a 3-4-3 to get another attacker up the field.

There is one exception to the numbers adding up to ten. If for any reason a team is playing with fewer than ten field players, as would be the case if a player got ejected, then the numbers would add up to that amount of field players. For example, a team playing with only nine field players might elect to play in a 4-4-1. Obviously, if your league doesn't play 11v11, your team's system won't add up to ten. In a 7v7 league, your team might play a 2-3-1.

A subset to system of play is how a team chooses to deploy each line of players. Defensively, a team can play with a flat back four (or 3) where its defenders are often in a flat line, or it may play with a sweeper who sits much deeper than her teammates. Some teams choose to play man-to-man defense, where each defender is assigned responsibility for shutting down one of the opponent's attackers. Many teams prefer to play a zonal defense where the individual defenders are responsible for an area of the field. Some teams use a combination of the two.

So when verbalizing a team's system like a true professional, you might say they play a 4-3-3, flat at the back; or you might say they play a 4-4-2, sweeper-stopper, man-to-man on the outside. Simple, yes?

If you're feeling pretty good about all this, you may want to throw the midfield shape into your assessment, such as: They play a 4-3-3, flat at the back, two low, one high in the middle.

Here's what you've just said: They play a flat back four (in which case 'zone' is implied), with 2 defensive center-midfielders, one attacking midfielder, and three forwards.

Nice work!

Check out the SocerPepper™ Lesson 6 video entitled *Systems*.

8

Styles

Style is the 'brand' of soccer a team plays. Commonly, at the youngest age groups, the only discernible style is *amoeba soccer, or bumblebee soccer*, where every player on the field runs around in a scrum surrounding the ball, like bees around the hive. But as players grow older and more technically competent, styles between teams will begin to diverge and reveal themselves.

Like a team's system, its style can change from one game to the next, or within a single game, based on a multitude of factors including the opponent, the field conditions, the score and the result needed. Also, a style is how a team *wants* to play. The opponent may not be very accommodating in allowing that to happen. The more outmatched your team is, the less likely you'll be able to impose your style on the game.

Let's look at some common styles of soccer.

INDIRECT AND DIRECT

Teams that play an indirect style are said to be *possession* teams or *passing* teams. They are not in a hurry to get the ball down to the opponent's goal and will frequently pass the ball sideways or backwards. Part of the strategy for playing indirect soccer is to wear down the opponent by making them chase the ball as you pass it from one player to the next. To get a better idea of what indirect soccer looks like, just watch any Barcelona possession video on Youtube. No team plays indirect soccer more convincingly than Barcelona.

Now that you know what indirect soccer is, you can probably guess what direct soccer looks like. Teams that play direct soccer are interested in quickly getting the ball to their highest player, or putting the ball in behind the opponent's line of defenders. There is much less lateral and negative (backward) passing, and more urgency to get the ball in front of the opponent's goal. At the younger age groups of youth soccer, we commonly see an uber-direct style of soccer known, disparagingly, as *kick-and-run*. Kick-and-run is exactly what it sounds like: a bunch of kids whacking the ball forward with no real plan other than advancing the ball toward the opponent's goal. At the professional level, direct soccer is much more structured and entertaining.

So why would a coach try to implement a direct style as opposed to an indirect style? Well, it all depends. It depends on the available players and the field conditions and the opponent. Plus, who's to argue with the idea of getting the ball near the opponent's goal as quickly as possible? Although indirect soccer is generally considered to be the more attractive style by soccer purists, either style, when well executed, can be very effective and fun to watch.

Much like deciding upon a system, a coach will design a team's style based on the available players. If a team has a couple of exceptionally fast forwards, it may be better served by whacking the ball in behind the opponent's defense and letting those speedsters go chase it. If a team has a big forward who is dominant in the air, it may want to flight balls into his head for flick-on headers that his teammates can run onto.

A team's style can also be the byproduct of external factors. A team may play direct soccer because the field conditions are poor, making it more difficult for players to control the ball. If you enjoy watching a team string together long runs of passes, indirect soccer can be prettier to watch, but it is also riskier. Trying to possess the ball can lead to more turnovers in dangerous areas. Typically, teams from wetter climates are more likely to play a more direct style because they need to get the ball in the air and above the puddles.

There are a multitude of factors a coach must consider when deciding the style of soccer his team will play. I've given you just a few of them. Believe me, there are many more.

Many teams play a blend of direct and indirect soccer, and sometimes that simply comes down to which player has the ball at any given moment. Some players are patient and want to slow the game down and possess the ball, but they may have teammates who are going to whack the ball 45 yards up the field every chance they get. A team's style is only as true as the players asked to play it.

Counter-Attack

The counter-attack style is typically a combination of low-pressure defending when the opponent has the ball and direct play when possession is won. The attacking idea behind this style is to draw the opponent out of its own end, which opens up the space in behind its defense. The objective is to win the ball in (or close to) your own half, then play forward quickly before a majority of the opponent's players have a chance to retreat into their defensive roles.

High-Pressure

High-pressure means chasing the ball regardless of where it is on the field, with the goal of forcing turnovers high up the field. A high-pressure style places a heavy physical demand on forwards who must relentlessly chase the ball when it is deep in the opponent's end.

Low-Pressure

A team that plays a low-pressure style of defense will wait for the opponent to move the ball up the field before engaging it in an effort to win possession. In basketball terms, high-pressure would look like a full-court press, while low-pressure would look more like a half-court defense. You won't see very many teams playing a low-pressure style at the youth level, but it is common at the professional level.

A team's style of play can change at any given moment, depending on the circumstances. For example, a high pressure team may elect to switch to a low pressure style if it is content to sit on a lead late in the game. Conversely, a low pressure team that is trailing will eventually be forced to start pressuring the opponent higher up the field in an effort to force turnovers. A team that normally plays indirect soccer may start playing much more directly if it is trailing late in the game and needs to get the ball up the field in a hurry.

A team's style is its default brand of soccer as established over a period of time. The more dominant a team is, the more likely it can stay true to its style.

9

Combination Play

I once heard that the more you know about something, the more interesting it becomes. I discovered the truth in that statement when I moved to Daytona Beach at the age of 29 and became immersed in a NASCAR culture. Prior to that, I was pretty ambivalent toward NASCAR. I didn't love it. I didn't hate it. I could take it or leave it. But once I started attending some races and learning about the cars and the drivers and the rabid fan base, the sport suddenly became a lot more interesting. Nothing about NASCAR changed, but my knowledge had grown immensely, and that made a huge difference in my perception. Before long I was spending a few Sundays each year in front of my television watching drivers make left turns for four straight hours... and loving it!

My point is this: The more you understand soccer, the more you will grow to love it. And I want to help. Combination play is one of soccer's shiniest jewels, particularly if you understand it. One look at a well-executed combination can give you an incurable case of love-at-first sight.

Combinations are a series of quick passes and movements designed to maneuver the ball through opponents. In a sport where aesthetics are revered almost as much as results, strong combination play gets high marks in both style and effectiveness. The successful execution of a combination is regarded as one of the prettiest pieces of play in the sport.

Is it critical for you to understand combination play? Absolutely not. But the game will become more enjoyable when you recognize that a combination has become available; and even more entertaining when the combination you foresee comes to fruition. Think of a game of checkers when you realize your opponent has just set you up for a quadruple jump of his pieces, just like you hoped he would. When you come to understand combination play, you'll see soccer as a checkerboard full of those potential multi-jump moments.

Instead of listing these alphabetically, we're going to go from basic, two-player combinations to advanced, three and four-player combinations. Also, because it will be a lot easier for you to understand these combinations by seeing them, be sure to check out the SoccerPepper™ video series with game footage of these combinations. Don't worry; I'll remind you again at the end of the chapter.

Wall Pass

The wall pass is also known as a *one-two* or a *give-and-go*. It is the most basic two-player combination in the sport. If you kicked a ball into a wall, it would bounce right back to you. In a wall pass, the second attacker serves as the wall.

Take-Over

The take-over is where a player dribbling in one direction leaves the ball for a teammate who is running in the opposite direction. It is very similar to a reverse in football, where the ball-carrier running east hands the ball off to a teammate who is running west.

Overlap

The overlap is where a player who is behind the ball-carrier makes a run to get in front of the ball-carrier to create a 2v1. The overlap is very similar to the option play in football, where the quarterback runs toward the sideline and then, based on the positioning of the opponent, either runs the ball up the field or laterals it to a teammate.

Underlap

The underlap is nearly identical to the overlap. In an overlap, the path of the overlapping player takes her wide of the ball-carrier (between the ball-carrier and the sideline). In an underlap, the underlapping player's run is to the inside of the ball-carrier (between the ball carrier and the middle of the field).

Up-Back-Through

The up-back-through combination is a three-player combination. The title of the combination explains the path of the ball. Typically, this combination begins with a ball being played *up* to a target forward who lays it *back* to a supporting player who then sends the ball *through* the defense for another teammate to run onto.

Third-Man Combo

Most commonly, the third man combination involves an overlap *and* some other pass or combination of passes. Specifically, the player being overlapped is not the one who passes the ball to the overlapping player. Typically the ball-carrier plays her pass toward the middle of the field to a teammate; that teammate is the one who ultimately plays the ball to the overlapping player. A successful third-man combo is one of soccer's prettiest combinations.

Check out the SoccerPepper™ Lesson 7 *Combinations* video.

10

What Not To Say

Now that you have a working soccer vocabulary and can understand some of the nuance of our sport, I would be remiss in my responsibility to your soccer-playing child if I didn't also give you some guidance as to what not to say. I suggest you follow my advice or risk embarrassing the heck out of your kid.

"Nice boot!"- Despite your best intentions, this is not actually a compliment, no matter how far or how high your child kicked the ball. As a matter of fact, no reference to distance or height will come off as complimentary to your child once he understands soccer. So avoid shouting things like *"Nice boot!"* and *"Good kick!"*

"Kick that ball!"- It goes without saying that this is what your daughter is trying to do anyway, but just kicking the ball doesn't separate a soccer player from any Schmoe off the street. A soccer player is actually trying to accomplish something beyond just putting her foot to the ball. If you want to encourage her, maybe just say, *"Go, Jenny!"* or *"Keep working!"*

"Nice header ball!"- Yeah, this is just a matter of semantics, but try this instead: *"Good header!"* Or maybe just go with, *"Well done!"* And by all means, never, under any circumstance, refer to it as *head-butting* the ball.

"Goaltender"- In soccer, the player that protects the goal is the goalkeeper or the goalie or the 'keeper, but not the goaltender.

"Shoot!!!"- When a player gets the ball in a goal-scoring position and is about to pull the trigger, he needs a calm mind. He needs to stay composed. His body needs to stay relaxed so that he may execute with the best possible technique. Twenty people screaming at Johnny to shoot is counterproductive to this process. It stresses Johnny out when everyone is screaming at him. Johnny knows to shoot. Just stay calm and let him be.

SECTION 2
WHAT YOUR
COACH WANTS
YOU TO KNOW

Anonymous Letter From A Volunteer Coach

*T*oday I heard a comment made about me behind my back. I started to turn around and look, but then decided better of it and kept my eyes on the field. My wife hears things like this more often than I do, because many of you don't know who she is. She tells me what you say.

I have received angry emails, full of 'suggestions,' about who should be playing where and how I lost that day's game for the kids. I thought I'd write an open letter to all of you parents, even though I might never send it.

I'll start it this way: I am a volunteer. I'm the one who answered the call when the league said they didn't have enough coaches. I understand that you were too busy. I have some news for you. I'm not retired. I'm busy too. I have other children and a job, just like you do. Not only do I not get paid to do this — it costs me money.

I see you walk up to the game 15 minutes after it started, still dressed for work. Do you know I've already been here for over an hour? Imagine if you had to leave work early nearly every day. I've never seen you at a practice. I'm sure you're plugging away at the office. But I'm out here, on the field, trying my best to teach these children how to play a sport they love, while my bank account suffers.

I know. I make mistakes. In fact, maybe I'm not even that great of a coach. But I treat the kids fairly and with respect. I am pretty sure they like coming to my practices and games, and without me or someone like me, there'd be no team for them to play on. I'm part of this community too and it's no picnic being out here on this stage like this. It's a lot easier back there with the other parents when no one is second guessing you.

And I also know you think I give my son unfair advantages. I try not to. In fact, have you ever considered that maybe I'm harder on him than the others? I'm sure he hears plenty of criticism at school from classmates, who hear it from you at home, about what a lame coach I am.

And if, even unconsciously, my kids are getting a slight advantage because I know them better and trust their abilities, is that the worst thing in the world, considering the sacrifice I'm making? Trust me, I want to win too. And if your son or daughter could guarantee we'd do that, I'd give them a chance.

After this game is over, I'll be the last one to leave. I have to break down the field, put away all the equipment and make sure everyone has had a parent arrive to pick them up. There have been evenings when my son and I waited with a player until after dark before someone came to get them.

Many nights I'm sure you've already had dinner and are relaxing on the couch by the time I finally kick the mud off my shoes and climb into my car, which hasn't been washed or vacuumed for weeks. Why bother cleaning during the season? Do you know how nice it would be if, just once, after a game one of you offered to carry the heavy gear bag to my car or help straighten up the field?

If I sound angry, I'm not. I do this because I love it and I love being around the kids. There are plenty of rewards and I remind myself that while you're at the office working, your kid is saying something that makes us all laugh or brings a tear to my eye. The positives outweigh the negatives. I just wish sometime those who don't choose to volunteer their time would leave the coaching to the few of us who do.

11

Social Problems

Now that you have a working vocabulary of what and what not to say, and an understanding of some of soccer's moving parts, you won't be totally lost when your daughter's team comes to your house after a game and the players start rambling on about that rotten offside call, or how the coach never should have switched them into a 4-4-2, or how Lisa got another yellow card. Congratulations! You're off to a running start. You're a semi-informed soccer parent. Don't worry about what you don't know yet. Go to your kid's games; watch a few Premier League matches on television. Before you know it, you'll be able to give a scouting report on next weekend's opponent.

But that's not why I wrote this book. I wrote this book so you won't be the reason that your child falls out of love with soccer. I've coached at the youth and college levels since 1991, so I've got a pretty good handle on what I'm talking about. I think I could sit here and tell you all there is to know about being a good, positive soccer parent just based on my own experience. But you deserve even more, so I went out and spoke to many other coaches, referees and even soccer-playing kids to get a more complete idea about how we can all be better soccer parents. So let me be perfectly clear: you have just entered the important part of the book. *You can have absolutely no knowledge of soccer and still be a great soccer parent.* And by that same token, you could have scored three goals in the World Cup and still be a rotten soccer parent. The good news is that the choice is entirely yours. I want to provide you with the relevant information you need to make an informed decision about the type of soccer parent you will choose to be.

Before we press on, let me remind you of the three major tenets behind the authorship of this book:

- *75% of kids quit playing by the age of 13.*
- *The number one reason they quit is because 'it stopped being fun.'*
- *PARENTS are a major reason it stopped being fun.*

My end-all, be-all goal for this book is to keep you from becoming a no-good, FUN-SUCKER. And before you think, *Ah, that'll never be me*, ask yourself how it's possible that nearly 8 out of every 10 kids quit. 75%! That's a huge number! Imagine if your kid took a test at school and got 75% of the answers wrong. Do you know what his grade would be? Of course you do! It would be a big, fat, stinkin' F. And it wasn't because he merely failed the test. Nope. He completely bombed it! And that's exactly the result we are producing as a nation of soccer parents. As a nation of soccer parents, our grade is a big, fat F written in bright, red ink.

Seventy-five percent. That's higher than the divorce rate, the dropout rate, the illiteracy rate and the poverty rate. It's higher than the number of people who ever try marijuana and higher than the number of people who will be involved in a car accident during their entire lifetime. Do you think it's because their parents intentionally sucked the fun out of the game for them? Of course not! Just like no one gets married expecting to divorce, and no one starts their car thinking that today is the day they get into an accident. Yet these things happen thousands of times each day from sea to shining sea. Here's my point: No parent intends to be a fun-sucker, yet it keeps happening, over and over and over again. Don't kid yourself into believing it could only happen to someone else.

I'm so happy you are reading this book because it means you're interested in solving the problem. It's a proactive step to becoming a wonderful, Gold Star Soccer Parent, and as a coach and a father, I applaud you for that.

Do me a favor... just keep an open mind and stick this out with me. Consider it a favor that you're doing because it's in your child's best interest, like when you gave up smoking or traded in your sports car for a minivan. You're going to hear from coaches, referees and most importantly, kids who play the game. Hear them out. What they say is going to surprise you. Some of it may even sting a little bit. Keep reading anyway. Keep reading because it's the right thing to do. Keep reading because your kid will be better off when you've finished this book.

Let's start with all those things your coach wants you to know.

12

Andy Reid And Yoko Ono

When I sent out an email to some coaching friends and told them that I was writing a book for soccer parents and would like suggestions, I wasn't surprised that my inbox immediately began filling up. I got an avalanche of responses within 30 minutes! Want to meet a group of people who have some things to get off their chests? Well then, I give you the youth soccer coaches of America. And they'd like to have a talk with you.

By and large, youth soccer coaches will sum up their experience with parents like this: *Most of the parents are awesome, but it just takes that one knucklehead to ruin your day.* I've heard coaches say those very words more times than I could possibly recall. It doesn't matter how well everything seems to be going, one misguided parent can torpedo a coach's morale and send it sinking to the ocean floor. Every coach has been there more times than you would believe, which is why so many of them were in a hurry to contribute to this book. They want their day in court. They want their chance to speak and be heard. They want to give you the chance to see some things from their perspective.

The parent/coach dynamic is a significant one. Do not underestimate the effect your attitude has on the bigger picture. As a soccer parent, make no mistake about it, you are an important part of the team. Whether you are important in a good way or a bad way, well, that's going to be up to you. But with a lot of help from some of this country's very best youth coaches, I'm going to point you in the right direction.

I think you would agree that it's in everyone's best interest, including your child's, that you have a positive relationship with your coach. Keep in mind that *positive* doesn't imply *close*. You can have a positive relationship and almost never cross paths. A lot of coaches would actually jump at that deal. *Positive* simply means that the two of you share a peaceful coexistence that is beneficial to both parties, and of course to your child. For that to happen, I'd like you to take a moment to look at things from your coach's perspective.

As a long-suffering Philadelphia Eagles fan, I was elated that we advanced to the 2004 Super Bowl, and I was even happier that with 46 seconds remaining we were only down by three points. And we had the ball! Okay, we were backed up to our own 4-yard line, but we still had a puncher's chance at pulling off a miracle.

On first down, with 96 long yards ahead of us, Donovan McNabb threw a screen pass to Brian Westbrook behind the line of scrimmage. Westbrook caught the ball for no gain and most of those 46 seconds burned off as we waited for everyone to return to the line of scrimmage so we could run the next play. It just went downhill from there. We looked like a team that had never even heard of a hurry-up offense, let alone a team that could run one.

If Westbrook had just dropped the ball instead of forcing a bad situation, the play would have been ruled an incomplete pass and almost no time would have run off the clock. Why did he catch that ball? Why did McNabb even throw him that ball? And why did we wait until that point in the game to go into hurry-up mode when we clearly should have been attacking with more urgency during the previous drive? The answer was obvious: *Andy Reid was an idiot.*

Yep, there I was, a guy who never played a single down of organized football, calling a professional football coach an idiot. Andy Reid had brought the Eagles franchise back from the dead and gotten us to the Super Bowl, but at that moment it didn't matter. *Andy Reid was an idiot.*

That's the thing about coaching – it's the one occupation that everyone feels qualified to do, and with a reasonable degree of certainty that they would do it better than the guy who currently holds the job. And this is the essence of what will drive a coach into an early retirement. I wouldn't dream of second guessing an engineer who was designing a bridge; I would never consider correcting the technique of a dentist as he drilled a tooth; I wouldn't even tell the vet how to clip my dog's nails. But on that night I was pretty darn confident that I could coach an NFL team to a Super Bowl victory over Bill Belichick, Tom Brady and the New England Patriots. Why do you think that is? Why do we all feel that we are qualified to be the coach?

Well, I don't know the answer to that, but I can tell you that as a coach, it's pretty frustrating, and not a day goes by that I don't offer Andy Reid a silent apology because I should have known better. I started playing soccer just before I turned seven-years-old. I played in four NCAA tournaments. I've coached college soccer for 23 years. I have an Advanced National Diploma from the NSCAA and an 'A' License from the USSF. I've helped develop players who went on to play in the Olympics and the World Cup. I've coached a dozen kids who went on to play professionally. But you can bet your backside that on any given day there's a parent in the stands who, despite having never kicked a ball in his life, will insist that I have no idea what I'm doing. This, my friend, is the life of a coach. And it's a major reason why a lot of excellent coaches refuse to coach youth soccer. Ask a good coach why he doesn't coach at the youth level and I guarantee you'll get this one-word answer: PARENTS.

That's right, kids aren't the only ones who quit because of fun-sucking parents. Coaches do too. All the time! Why? Because it's just not worth it. Because there are more enjoyable ways to spend our time. Because there are plenty of other thankless jobs waiting to be filled. But mostly because Paul McCartney doesn't want a critique of his vocals from Yoko Ono. And chances are, you're Yoko Ono.

It's in your best interest - *and in your kid's best interest* - to get the best possible coaching from the best possible coaches. That won't happen if you keep running them off. So let's take a look at things from your coach's point of view and see if we can bridge the gap between what he's doing and what you *think* he's doing.

13

Releasing Your Child

Having a positive relationship with your coach is really easy. Think of it as a *less is more* proposition. The less you interfere, the more your coach can accomplish.

Generally speaking, a coach's biggest concern for parents is that they don't undermine what he is trying to build. And yes, it most certainly is a building process. Coaches know that a team is like a Jenga tower – it is a lot easier to destroy than it is to build, and if the wrong beam comes loose, the foundation will crumble. Coaches have enough fires to put out without parents running around lighting matches. A coach's job is impossible to fully comprehend unless you've done it and done it for a while.

If your child is going to get more from soccer than just soccer skill, then you have to release him to his coach. For a few hours a day, a few days a week, you've got to turn your kid over to the coach and trust that the coach is doing what's right. But remember, doing what is right isn't always synonymous with making your kid 100% happy 100% of the time.

You don't sit next to your son in the classroom. You already release your child to his teachers five days a week. That shouldn't change just because your son puts on a shiny soccer jersey and faces a win-lose situation on Saturday mornings. Your son's coach is also his teacher. You've got to give that teacher the freedom to do what he has been hired, or more likely, *volunteered* to do. If you don't, you're going to cheat your child out of the experience he should be having.

To be a Gold Star Soccer Parent, you have to understand what soccer is, and also, what it is not. Soccer is a competition. Even at the youngest ages where soccer should be participation-oriented and not results-oriented, there is still a hierarchy being formed. Some players are going to be better than others. Some kids just have better coordination and balance. Some just have a gift. Soccer is not the sandbox of equality. Yes everyone can play, but some will play better than others.

Let's say there are two six-year-old boys who are clones in terms of physical attributes, and let's say that neither of those boys has ever kicked a soccer ball, and let's say we signed them up to be on the same soccer team. If those two boys went through the exact same soccer practices and games for a whole year, and neither boy did anything extra outside of the organized practices, at the end of that year, one of those boys is going to be better than the other one. There could be a hundred reasons why, but the bottom line is that one child had a greater natural affinity for the game. And that player inches his way higher up soccer's food chain.

Try to remember that the foundation of all competition is to find a winner. That's it. Even if your child isn't playing at a level that emphasizes results, even if participation is the end-all be-all priority of his coach and his league, the element of competition can't be entirely erased. At soccer practices your child will engage in any number of exercises that involve competing, and that means someone has to win. Of course if there's going to be a winner, there must also be a loser. And on any given day, your child will lose, and lose multiple times. That's okay. It's better than okay. It's freaking fantastic because it gives your child the chance to respond to adversity! And it gives you the opportunity to nudge him in the right direction when choosing his response.

My point is this: soccer shouldn't always be a bowl of cherries. Soccer should be a challenge. It should test your child on a physical, mental and emotional level. I've got a nine-year-old daughter that plays soccer and if she always comes home 100% happy, then something is wrong. I don't want her to always be over-the-moon happy. For soccer to be rewarding, it has to be more than just fun. If I wanted Izzy to simply have fun every day, I would just buy her a season pass to Six Flags. I expect a little bit more from soccer. I want soccer to challenge her into making admirable responses to situations both good and bad.

The best advice I ever got on parenting came almost a decade before I ever became a parent: *You're not raising a child; you're raising an adult.* I love that saying and I try to let it guide me through those difficult times when I have to decide whether to rescue Izzy or let her fight her own battle. I have to remember that survival is the ultimate life skill, and competition via soccer provides a consistent and relatively safe platform for her to demonstrate her ability to face adversity, persevere and survive.

I want Izzy to learn more from soccer than just how to dribble, pass and shoot a ball. I want it to test her as a player, a person and a teammate. Some days I want it to knock her down just so she has to get back up — just so she learns that she *can* get back up. My kid having a bad day at soccer is not the world's worst tragedy. Sometimes it's even worth celebrating. I know that the battles she fights, and even the ones she loses, will all shape her into becoming a well-adjusted, self-reliant adult. And that's what I'm ultimately trying to raise.

So keep that in mind when your son comes home and is distraught because his coach criticized him in front of his teammates or because he didn't get to be in the starting line-up. It doesn't automatically mean that the coach was wrong or that the coach isn't good. It's all part of the process. You can find victory even in these defeats. You just need to know where to look.

Remember that you and the coach ultimately share the same goal: to serve your child's best interests. The two of you are just taking separate paths to get there. For your child to get more out of soccer than just soccer, you have to start by releasing him to his coach.

14

Evaluating Your Coach

Having the right coach is critical to your child's overall experience, but keep this in mind: From your child's perspective, having a coach he enjoys can, and most often will, be more important than the team's results. Kids are more concerned with enjoying themselves than with winning or losing. Thankfully, many leagues mandate coaching education courses for their coaches. It's a good start, but it's not a magic wand solution. A volunteer with no soccer or coaching background can only learn so much from a four-hour course. Volunteer coaches are learning as they go. Try to keep your expectations in perspective when you are dealing with a coach who is just learning the game, particularly when he's doing it for free.

Do you have the right to evaluate your coach? Absolutely. *Within limits.* You have the right to know that your coach is not abusing your child mentally, emotionally or physically; and you have the right and responsibility to intervene immediately if you have good reason to suspect anything of the sort. You have the right to expect that your coach is looking out for the best interests of your child's physical welfare. If your coach is holding practice under a sky full of lightning bolts, you've got a responsibility to speak up. And you have the right to expect your coach to do his best to develop the players and further their passion for the game.

I'm not going to pretend that every soccer coach out there is a good one. There are good coaches and there are plenty of bad ones. But when evaluating your coach, you've got to make sure you are using the proper criteria. Winning doesn't automatically make a coach good and losing doesn't automatically make him bad. I wish I could give you a blanket statement for thoroughly evaluating your coach, but that's not realistic. However, these five questions should give you a running start:

- *Is the coach concerned about my child's physical, mental and emotional safety?*
- *Is his behavior setting a good example for my child?*
- *Do training sessions focus on the technical development of the players?*
- *Are the players being challenged?*
- *When one soccer practice/game ends, does my child look forward to the next one?*

If you answer 'no' to these questions, it may be time to start looking for a new team or coach. If you can answer 'yes' to these five questions, then chances are you've got yourself a pretty decent coach. Now let's see what we can do to keep him.

15

Understand Your Coach's Philosophy And Goals

To evaluate your coach, you have to understand his philosophy and his goals. You need to know exactly what he is trying to accomplish. Most coaches are very happy to share these things with anyone who will listen, and usually you'll get more than you bargained for.

Winning is great and we all agree it's a long cry better than the alternative, but judging your child's season, or your child's coach, on wins and losses might be a giant mistake. Can I share a little secret with you? Winning a game of soccer at the U-8 level is pretty irrelevant in life's grand scheme. Frankly, when dealing with children up until the age of about 13, a coach should have two primary practice objectives for his players:

- *They improve as soccer players, particularly in their technical ability*
- *They want to come back to the next practice*

If the coach is meeting one of those objectives, then chances are he is also meeting the other one. The more kids play, the more they improve. The more they improve, the more they want to play. And in case you didn't already do the math, if they are playing more and developing more at the younger levels, guess what's going to start happening pretty quickly as they get older. That's right, the results will follow.

Don't judge your coach based on wins and losses, because winning might not be one of his top priorities. Let me give you some excellent advice: if your kid is nine-years-old and the coach puts all of his emphasis on player development, you've got yourself a keeper. If your kid is nine-years-old and the coach's number one priority is to win, start looking for a new team.

Here's a little secret that soccer coaches have known since forever ago: The most technical and smartest players are often the slowest. Would you like to know why? Because fast players spend their formative years solving their soccer problems with speed. But the slower ones have to find another way to survive and advance up the pyramid. They have to adapt to their environment. They do that by developing their technical ability and their soccer IQ. It's soccer's Darwinism.

It's very easy to win games at the younger age groups when you have fast players. There's no tremendous accomplishment in that. But eventually, as players' bodies change, the kids who dominated with speed up to the age of 12 suddenly aren't so much faster than everybody else. Now they need something more than speed to solve their soccer problems. Hopefully, for their sake, they had coaches who prioritized skill development over winning.

Years ago I was at a showcase recruiting tournament looking at college prospects. This was back when these tournaments used to work a lunch break into the schedule. During the lunch break I wandered over to a field where a local U-6 league was having a game of 5v5. I thought it would be a nice change of pace to watch the little tikes doing their thing.

On my honor, I left after five minutes. It was frightening! The parents were so involved in the game, so invested in the result, that it scared me to think of what might happen. They yelled and screamed and jumped up and down and yelled and screamed some more. Who could worry so much about which team of five-year-olds won a soccer game? I mean, who cares?

I am the most competitive person I know. I am not driven by winning; I am driven by an unholy need to avoid losing. It's what makes me tick and always has. So please believe me when I say that in this country, we put entirely too much emphasis on winning soccer games at the lower youth levels, and it costs us dearly when those players are older. Let me repeat myself: If you are judging your eight-year-old son's coach on how many games the team wins or loses, you aren't doing anyone any favors.

I once spoke with a highly respected youth coach from Europe who had spent some time in the U.S. observing our soccer culture, and he was stunned by the emphasis we put on winning at the youngest ages. He said the single, biggest problem with youth soccer in the United States was that we evaluate youth coaches on wins and losses. He told me that in Europe, youth coaches were ultimately judged by how many of their players went on to play professionally. Think about that for a second. If we judged our coaches on how successful their players became years on down the road, wouldn't that free up the coaches to spend more time on actually developing the players instead of worrying about winning? Of course it would.

You need to understand your coach's goals before you can judge whether or not she is reaching those goals. In addition to player development, her goals may be heavily weighted toward character development or teamwork or any of those other qualities that will eventually matter more than whether or not your kid won the U-9 championship. Winning feels great in the short-term, but you've got to remember that there are bigger fish to fry. If you've got a coach who wants to focus on player development, don't talk her out of it.

16

Avoid Basing Your Relationship On Soccer

Every few years I coach a player who is on the bubble of being or not being in the starting line-up. Let's call her Kristen. Some games Kristen is on the field for 60 or 70 minutes. Some games she doesn't play at all. After the game, as I'm walking off the field, if Kristen played a bunch of minutes, her mom and dad are all smiles and hugs and handshakes. It doesn't matter if we won or lost; Kristen played a lot of soccer and that means on that night, her parents think I'm aces. When Kristen gets playing time, I'm a great coach. However, on those nights when Kristen doesn't play, her parents go out of their way to let me know they want nothing to do with me. They position themselves so I'll have to walk right by them, but they won't say a word. They'll just tilt down their chins and shake their heads to convey the message that I've really failed them. It's a childish response and it certainly doesn't impact my decision on whether or not Kristen will play in the next game. I'm going to do what I feel is in my team's best interest, no matter how convincing the parents are at conveying their disappointment.

Kristen's parents base our relationship on soccer games and soccer games only. They evaluate our relationship 90 minutes at a time. If you want to be a Gold Star Soccer Parent, I really hope you'll avoid this.

If you base the coach-parent relationship solely on soccer, I guarantee you that you're going to end up disappointed. Soccer is a fickle sport. You are going to win some and you're going to lose some and you're going to lose some that you should have won. That's life. How I value Kristen as a human being has nothing at all to do with her playing time. And her soccer ability has nothing to do with how I value her as a person. Don't be the parent who assigns value to my relationship with your child based on the amount of minutes she gets on a soccer field. It's just silly and it puts everyone, including your daughter, in an awkward position.

Remember that the player-coach relationship is much more than what you see during a game. At the college level, when I see your daughter more than you do, I am looking out for her best interest in ways that have almost nothing to do with soccer. I might be monitoring her grades and encouraging her in the class-room; I might be the guy she comes to when her boyfriend is being a pinhead; and there's an excellent chance that somewhere down the line she's going to ask me to write her a letter of recommendation. I will do all of these things for her regardless of whether she plays 90 minutes a game or never plays at all. Because that's what coaches do.

At the younger age groups, your coach is helping in other ways. He's looking for ways to build your son's confidence and to help him fit into the group. He's giving him advice about soccer and school and the science fair. He's teaching him about courage and respect and hard work and sportsmanship. And when it rains, he's probably giving up his jacket so your son can stay dry.

There really is more to life than playing time and wins or losses. Your child and coach have a relationship that you will never fully know or understand. The good coach doesn't base that relationship on your son's soccer ability. You shouldn't either. Strive to maintain a consistent and even-keel relationship regardless of the scoreboard or playing time. You don't necessarily have to be happy about those things, but they shouldn't affect your interactions with anyone on the coaching staff.

17

No Sideline Coaching

If we made a list of complaints that youth coaches have about parents, this would be right near the top, mainly because so many parents can't seem to help themselves once the game begins. We are so eager to help our kids succeed in the competitive arena, and so afraid that they might be conquered, that we pepper them with advice from the sideline. There are two people who strongly prefer that you refrain from sideline coaching: your kid and your coach. Later on we'll talk about this from your child's point of view; for now we'll just focus on the coach.

There is a difference between cheering and coaching. *Cheering* means expressing your joyful emotion in the moments after something has gone well, or providing encouragement as the game goes on. *Coaching* means giving advice as the play is developing or providing correction after it has happened. Cheering is good. Coaching is bad. Here's why:

Let's start by saying you either have a strong soccer background or you don't. If you don't, then it doesn't make much sense to be advising your child when it comes to soccer. Let's face it; if you had no background in repairing cars, you wouldn't stand in the garage telling the mechanic how to fix your transmission. And you wouldn't want someone else with no automotive background telling the mechanic what to do either. And you sure as heck wouldn't want the mechanic taking advice from that novice! Why? Because when your mechanic takes advice from people who have never worked under the hood, he's going to destroy your transmission!

If you don't have a strong soccer *playing* background, make peace with the fact that you just don't have enough soccer knowledge to be helpful. Unfortunately, you're just unqualified, so you really have no idea if what you're saying is right or wrong. And the last thing in the world your coach wants you to do is give bad advice to his players. I've been coaching for more than two decades and every now and then I still give my players a piece of bad advice during the run of play. If I still make mistakes, what are the chances that you won't make a lot more of them? It doesn't matter how badly you want to help your team succeed, you've got to refrain from coaching because you're going to do more harm than good.

But what if you actually do have a strong soccer background? Well, this is a little bit trickier because convincing *you* not to be a sideline coach is even more difficult. You are convinced that you have something to offer, and you may be right. So what do you do?

Zip it.

That's right, in spite of your expertise which may be genuinely grand, remember that you are not the coach and then showcase your exceptional willpower by biting your tongue.

But why?

A team needs to be led by a single voice. There ultimately needs to be one decision-maker, and on game day, no one should be competing with that voice when it comes to providing instruction. Sideline coaches are radio static. They clog the communication lines with white noise and they confuse and distract the players.

You don't know what the coach wants. You don't know what objectives he has set for his team aside from winning the game. Anything you say as a sideline coach has an excellent chance of contradicting what the coach has already asked of his players. Let me give you some examples.

Johnny is playing right wing and has the ball at midfield. He can easily pass the ball to Bill who is running up the field, and because you have the soccer background to see this, you shout at Johnny to pass the ball to Bill. And he does. Johnny made a good, unselfish pass that helped his team in the short term. So what's the problem? Your advice was correct, right? Well, sometimes you can be right and still be wrong. And in this hypothetical, you just were.

Coach believes Johnny can develop into an excellent 1v1 attacker, but right now Johnny lacks confidence. Lately at practice, Coach has been working with Johnny on his 1v1 skills and thinks that this particular game against this particular opponent will be an excellent opportunity for Johnny to develop his 1v1 attacking confidence. Before the match, Coach told Johnny that whenever he was matched up against a single defender, Johnny was to try to dribble past that defender. And he also told all of Johnny's teammates what he expected of Johnny and how this would help the team in the long run. So when Johnny got the ball and faced that defender, the voice in his head was telling him, *"My job right now is to try to beat this guy on the dribble."* But stomping all over that voice was your voice, shouting at Johnny to pass the ball, and your voice trumped Coach's voice and in that moment, neither Johnny nor his team got any better.

Sideline parents make these mistakes all the time. They tell a player to pass when the coach wants him to dribble; or they tell him to dribble when the coach wants him to pass. They tell a defender to stay back when the coach wants her to get forward. They'll scream at Mia to shoot the free kick from 35 yards when the coach prefers that she put it up in the air for Abby to head.

It doesn't matter how qualified you are, please don't coach someone else's team. You don't have enough information. You don't have access to the big picture. You don't know what's been going on at training and you don't know what the coach asked of his players before the game began. Because you don't have access to this information, anything you say might contradict what the coach is trying to accomplish. So instead of coaching, just sit back and enjoy watching your kid play soccer. And when he does something well, say, *"Nice job!"*

And if you just can't stop yourself from being a sideline coach, here's some fantastic advice: Next season, when the league is searching for volunteer coaches, sign on. Leagues everywhere are starving for coaches with actual soccer knowledge. Then you can coach, coach, coach all you want and the kids will be better for it.

18

Tactics And Personnel

During my college days I took a job bartending in a brand new restaurant. The owner was a fantastic and friendly gentleman who always made time to have a few words with the customers. As many of these conversations took place at the bar, I was privy to overhearing quite a few of them. In the first month we opened, the most common phrase I heard from the customers was, *"Do you know what you should do?"* It didn't just happen once in a while; it was a total epidemic. Here was a guy who spent an awful lot of time and money to realize his dream of opening a restaurant that served great food; he was working his tail off 18 hours a day and all anyone wanted to tell him is what he should be doing differently.

Eventually the litany of suggestions wore him down and he finally vented about it. He was doing his darndest to deliver a great dining experience, but all of these comments were suggesting that in some form or fashion, he should be doing more. No one saw all the work he was putting in each and every day; no one knew the challenges he was facing. But everyone wanted to tell him how to do it better.

My point is this: Your coach wants your support, but not necessarily your input. I can assure you that if your coach wants your opinion on tactics, she'll let you know. If she doesn't come to you, then it's safe to assume she's not looking for your opinion. Offering unsolicited advice is a bad move because it cuts on a personal level. It suggests a degree of incompetence. I mean, would you want someone showing up at your office and advising you on how to do a better job of whatever it is you do? Wouldn't you feel insulted if someone with no practical background, someone who has never done what you do, started telling you how you could do your job more effectively? When you start offering unsolicited, tactical suggestions, you are insulting your coach. Believe it.

When I asked youth coaches to contribute their thoughts to this book, every single one of them mentioned unsolicited advice from parents as a major source of disenchantment.

You have to understand that there are things you don't know, and that there might be a very good reason you don't know them. I'll give you an example from a friend of mine who coaches college women. Here's the story as he tells it:

Years ago I was on the coaching staff at another university and we decided to start Player B over Player A in an important game, even though Player A was clearly the better player.

Sure enough, we lost the game and our shot at a conference championship. Suddenly everyone with a passing interest in our team decided we were idiots because Player A didn't get on the field. They were certain that had she played, we would have won. And you know what? They were probably right.

However, what no one knew was that Player A had developed a serious medical condition. Not even her parents were aware of it yet. If word had gotten out, it would have been horribly awkward for her. Out of respect for her privacy, we weren't going to advertise why she wasn't playing. As far as we were concerned, it was nobody else's business. And we were right. Still, the critics lined up to tell anyone who would listen that we didn't know what the heck we were doing.

Think about that for a second. From our perspective, we were doing the player a favor by protecting her privacy and saving her from an extremely uncomfortable situation. We knew we were acting in the player's best interest. We knew we were doing the right thing. But from the outside looking in, all you could see was a pair of dimwits. Of course it made a lot more sense the next day when she told her parents that she was pregnant.

I know, right? How's that for a twist?

Everything is not always as it seems.

Not many examples will be that extreme, but you still have to accept that you are an outsider and that there are things you don't know. You don't know who is injured or to what extent; you don't know who is having a discipline issue; you don't know who has been goofing off at practice or who has been coming on strong. You don't have access to a fraction of the information that your coach has. All you see is the product presented.

So, once again, for your sake, I gently ask that you refrain from volunteering your tactical suggestions. It will be perceived as horribly insulting, and it's even worse immediately after a loss. As badly as the spirit is moving you to say something, don't. Just bite your tongue and skip that topic.

You're going to have some heavy emotions immediately after a game. By now you probably know that making decisions in an emotionally volatile state is rarely a good idea. If you have to say something, give yourself a 24-hour cool down period. Give your thermometer a chance to get back to room temperature before you write that email. And incidentally, I highly recommend an email instead of a phone call. You can edit and re-edit your email. You can polish it until it shines with tact and diplomacy. You can have someone else critique your work for potentially inflammatory language. You won't be overcome with the emotion of a heated exchange. And after you've written it all out, you can even sleep on it. A day later you might choose not to send it. On the phone, you've got no such luxury. Once it comes out of your mouth, there's no getting it back.

Email also gives the coach a chance to digest your words and to hold off on an immediate, emotional response. When you call a coach in a moment like this, from where the coach is sitting, it feels a lot like an ambush. Anyone who is ambushed is going to get defensive and you're not going to get his best response. Email gives you both a more emotionally stable vehicle for having an adult conversation, and you can even use email to set up a phone call or a face-to-face meeting.

Some of the most prominent clubs in the country have a policy that prohibits parents from contacting a coach within 24 hours of a game's conclusion. That's a brilliant policy and one I hope that every club/league/team adopts. A good night's sleep and some hindsight always help to put things into perspective.

No one is his best self in the moments after a defeat. Don't let your emotions get the better of you. Don't take a bad situation and make it worse. Take some deep breaths, count to ten and then give yourself a day to cool off. For something productive to occur, you need to do more than just vent.

Since we are talking about communicating with your coach, please also refrain from offering suggestions for practice topics. The coach watched the same game you did, so he's pretty aware of your team's strengths and weaknesses. Because he's the coach, it's his puzzle to solve. No matter how you present it, he's going to feel slighted by your lack of faith in his ability, just like my friend who opened the restaurant. If you really want to design soccer practices, I'll once again nudge you to volunteer your services at the Rec. Department.

There's no gentle way for me to say this next one, so I'm just going to put it out there for you. Never, under any circumstance, submit your suggestion for the starting line-up or formation. If there were a list of soccer parent commandments, this one would be at the top. When you hand that sheet of paper to the coach, what you're saying is that he isn't qualified to decide who should be playing where. As you can probably imagine, that won't go over so well. Deciding who plays where is the coach's job and nobody else's.

And finally, when a game is in progress, don't text the coach your suggestions for tactics or personnel. (It scares me that I even need to mention this.) A parent who does this is overstepping his boundaries in epic fashion.

If you want to be a coaching asset to your team, volunteer your services, preferably at the very beginning of the season, before the team starts playing games. Politely introduce yourself to the coach and say something like, *"I don't know if you want any help, but I actually played soccer in high school and I'd be happy to help out if you need anything."* Plenty of youth coaches have no soccer background whatsoever and are thrilled to take on a partner.

Incidentally, if your coach is your coach because he volunteered, then I'm going to ask that you ease up on the criticisms. Don't expect a volunteer coach to have a vast understanding of the sport. He probably took the job so his kid would have a team to play on, and because he did, your kid has a team to play on also. Use this knowledge to make peace with the many imperfections he will demonstrate as he learns the game and how to coach it.

When it comes to volunteers, we have to take the bad with the good. Volunteers make up 80% of the youth coaching community. They keep the soccer world spinning and we need to protect them like we would an endangered species. Do your part to keep the volunteers coming back.

19

Playing Time Issues

I once heard a coaching school instructor say that eventually everyone reaches a level where they are no longer good enough to play. I had never thought of it that way, but it made perfect sense. If it wasn't true, I would be playing for our national team which, incidentally, would have a roster of millions. Eventually we're just not good enough. And that applies to each and every one of us.

But what about Lionel Messi? Yes, the same thing applies to Messi. The world's best player won't be good enough to play for Barcelona or Argentina or even the Rochester Rhinos twenty years from now. Eventually, even world-class players age out.

Soccer participation is a competitive pyramid. The lowest level of competition has the most participants. The very highest level, the national team level, has the fewest. The higher you go up the pyramid, the harder it is to hang on. And at each vertical step there is a new coach deciding whether or not you get to keep climbing. Why? Because eventually someone has to decide who plays, who sits, and who doesn't make the team. That role falls to a coach.

The selection process is much simpler in sports with an objective mechanism for evaluation like track or swimming. In swimming, it's easy to identify the best swimmer because he's the one with the best time. The second-best swimmer has the second-best time and so on down the line. It's hard to argue with that measuring stick. Swimming coaches don't have to justify their hierarchy because a stopwatch does that for them. In soccer, the evaluation is a much more subjective process. It's up to the coach to evaluate the talent and decide which players are better than other players – because somebody has to. This subjectivity has been the undoing of many parent/coach relationships.

As you ponder playing time, figure out why your child is playing soccer. If his objective is to make a career from the game, then he's going to have to keep scaling that pyramid. The higher he climbs, the more likely he is to fail. But if your son's objective is to play simply because he loves playing, he should have no trouble finding a place to play. Once your soccer player reaches a certain age and level of competitive soccer, he'll be on a team that owes him nothing, including playing time. What I'm trying to say is that if your child isn't getting the playing time he craves, maybe he just needs to slide back down the pyramid a little bit. The day may come where you have to put your ego aside and accept the fact that to meet his need for playing time, he may have to drop down a level. Don't pretend that's not an option. Don't let your ego cloud your vision or you're going to end up banging your head against a very hard wall. Your kid wants to play soccer, not watch it. Put him in a position to get on the field.

Playing time is the brass ring of any sport and soccer is no exception. Coaches understand how badly players want to play and how badly they want to be part of the starting line-up and how strongly a child's identity can be tied into his athletic prowess. We know your child would be happier if he started and played every minute, and we would love to make every child as happy as he could be, but unfortunately, being a coach isn't like being Santa Claus. You see, there is a serious math problem we have to contend with. There are only so many players allowed on the field at any given time, and the game is only so many minutes long.

A friend of mine was once having issues with his college team as some of the players were becoming disgruntled with their lack of playing time. To address the situation, my friend called a team meeting and gave each player a sheet of paper. Each player was asked to write down her name and the number of minutes she felt she deserved to play based on her ability.

There were 26 field-players in the room (goalkeepers were excluded). Some players were on a full-scholarship; some players received no scholarship money; and most fell somewhere in between. My friend collected all those sheets of paper and added up the totals. As expected, some players wrote that they should be playing 90 minutes; some wrote 75 or 60 or 40 or 20. No one wrote down 0. There were 26 players in the room and *every single one of them* felt she deserved to be playing at least 20 minutes.

The coach then explained to them that there are 10 field-players on the field at any given time, and that a soccer game is 90 minutes long. That means there are 900 available man-minutes. The total number of minutes the players felt they deserved added up to nearly 1700! That's almost double the amount of available minutes! Can you see a little disconnect there?

Stranger still, some players who never cracked the line-up felt they should be playing the entirety of every match. Whereas the coach felt they weren't talented enough to warrant any playing time, these players felt they should be playing every minute of every game. Doesn't that strike you as somewhat peculiar? This is what coaches are dealing with. A player's perception of her competitive value does not always align itself with reality. The same can be said for the perceptions of her parents.

It's a little bit easier at the college level because we don't have to contend with league rules that say every kid has to play a quarter or a half, and parents aren't paying money for their daughters to be on our team. Nobody is guaranteed playing time, so we don't have to deal with those types of entitlement issues. We get paid to win games and if we don't win enough of them, we get fired. This keeps our perspective very clear. That doesn't mean we don't have to occasionally deal with some unhappy players; it's just that we don't feel obligated to entertain them when they fuss.

When you're tempted to complain about playing time, remember this: *Coaches evaluate talent.* That is the coach's job and nobody else's. Now you might not agree with his conclusions, but that's just how the cookie crumbles. It's not your job; it's his. As long as your child is getting on the field for the minimum amount guaranteed by league rules, you are getting everything that you are realistically entitled to get.

But Dan, my kid is the best player on the team! She should be playing more!

Oh, I absolutely agree with you. This is how I know.

In addition to my job of coaching at the University of Georgia, I am also our summer soccer camp administrator. That means, among other things, I answer the phone. Between February and July, that phone rings an awful lot. As you might expect, many of those calls are from parents who want to know a little bit more about our camp before signing up their child. I've fielded thousands of phone calls and the number of parents who tell me their kid is the best player on his/her team is absolutely staggering. For starters, it is truly fascinating that so many people can even work that premise into a conversation! It's led me to the conclusion that every parent genuinely believes his kid is the best player on the team. There's no other viable explanation. And I totally get it! It's the same as every parent believing that their baby is the cutest one in the history of procreation. And it's no different than a reserve player feeling that she deserves to play 90 minutes a game. If players can be so misguided, then why would we expect any different from their parents?

Listen to me because this is important: *You aren't objective.* You can't be. You can't disconnect yourself from your child to the point of total objectivity. It's literally impossible. That's why your team has a coach. Can you imagine if, for just one game, the line-up was decided by a meeting of all the parents? Do you have any idea how long it would take to finalize a starting line-up and the playing time for each player? Can you imagine the body count? It would be utter chaos! What parent is going to stand there and say, *"Well I don't think my kid should be starting?"* Would *you* do that?

One of the standard playing-time complaints from parents is that the coach plays favorites. I totally agree with you on that, one-thousand percent! I definitely have my favorites. I've had favorites since the day I started coaching. You know who my favorites are? They're the kids who work the hardest and give my team the best chance to win the game. I absolutely love those kids! That's why they start and that's why they play the most minutes.

If you want to give your child a recipe for playing a lot of minutes, here it is in two, simple words: *Outwork everyone.* If your child legitimately outworks everyone every time she goes to the soccer field, she's going to get a lot of playing time because she's going to be one of the coach's favorites. All coaches love the players who work tirelessly to improve, compete and win, because they lend value to our existence. They are the ones who keep us excited about coming back!

Do your daughter a favor. Don't ever tell her that she would play more if the coach wasn't playing favorites. It's not helping you and it's hurting your kid. There is a lot more to sports than just being happy. Sports are a wonderful meritocracy where the best are rewarded with the most. Sports should challenge your child. If your child never experiences any type of emotional discomfort through soccer, then something is very wrong. If she is 100% happy 100% of the time, she's not being challenged nearly enough. But the great thing about sports is that they give participants a chance to respond, a chance to prove themselves. If your child complains about her playing time, don't jump on board as her campaign manager because you won't be doing her any favors. When your kid is unhappy with her playing time, she has a choice to make: Surrender or dig in.

Would you like a stellar response for those moments when your child is disenchanted with her playing time? Tell your daughter to *prove him wrong*. Tell her to work even harder at practice, *and away from it*, to prove to the coach that he is wrong and that she should be on the field.

Prove him wrong is a fantastic response because it allows you to take your child's side without undermining the coach, and it still puts the responsibility on your child to make a choice about how she is going to respond to her current adversity. Incidentally, this is pretty good practice for life in general.

If none of what you've just read has convinced you not to obsess about your child's playing time, then maybe this story will. Again, this involves college players.

Many years ago I coached a defender who had been a regular starter for her first two years. But in her junior year we had brought in a very talented freshman who played the same position. I knew it was only a matter of time before the freshman won the spot, but I didn't want to just hand it over; I wanted to make the freshman earn it.

The freshman was a fantastic kid. She worked hard every day at practice. She never complained. She was a great teammate. She said and did all the right things, and with each passing week I would reward her with a little more playing time. Well, finally the day had come. I was about to head out to practice where I would announce our starting line-up for the next night's game. The freshman was about to get her first start as a college soccer player and she had earned every bit of it.

I was halfway out of my office when the desk phone rang. To this day I'm still kicking myself for answering it. It was the freshman's father, confronting me about his daughter being left out of the starting line-up. Clearly I didn't know what I was doing and he was calling to set me straight. In that moment that father had become his daughter's campaign manager, and even though he had wonderful intentions for his girl, his plan backfired mightily.

Dad hadn't thought this one all the way through before he picked up the phone. He never stopped to consider the position he was about to put me into. Now there was no way on earth for me to put his daughter in the starting line-up. If she started that game, inevitably the rest of the world would find out and think that it was because her father had demanded it. I wasn't about to set that precedent! My phone would have been ringing off the hook with parents trying to bully their kid into the starting line-up!

With one phone call that father took his kid off the field. Don't make that same mistake.

Coaches have to be very concerned about setting dangerous precedents. Coaches are the ones responsible for holding an unmovable line when it comes to the team's standards. What applies to one must apply to all and we just can't afford to let certain toothpaste out of the tube. Recognize when you're about to box your coach into a corner. Take a moment to step back and see the whole picture. Give your kid a chance to fight her own battles and she just might surprise you.

Incidentally, your daughter doesn't want playing time because her father hounded the coach. There's no reward in that. Sure she wants to play, but she wants to play because she earned it. When your daughter fights her way into the line-up, she wants to know it's because of the work she put in to get there. And when that day comes, she'll be proud of it, and you will be proud of her.

The higher your child climbs up the soccer pyramid, the more you must be prepared for her to eventually plateau, because somewhere on the way up, results trump participation. Eventually having a team full of happy players is no longer a coach's concern. Winning and losing become the priority because results determine whether the coach keeps or loses his job. Being the best player on the rec team doesn't mean your kid should be starting at the club or high school level. And being the best player on her high school team guarantees your daughter nothing once she reaches the college level.

College soccer is pretty high up on that competitive pyramid, so it's where a lot of players reach the end of the line in terms of playing time. It seems that once every few years we have a player step forward to complain about her playing time. This has been going on since I first started coaching in 1991, so I've had a lot of time to polish up my response. These days, this is what I tell them:

No one has a right to playing time. Playing time is something you earn. The players who give us the best chance of winning are going to start and they're going to play the most minutes and your coaches get to decide who those players are. Now look, no one forced you to come to this university. You knew that you could go to a smaller school and be a starter and play 90 minutes a game and be a total rock star, but you wanted to challenge yourself at the highest level. So you chose to come here. That was your choice and you knew full well that you would have to compete against some of the best players in the country for playing time. The fact of the matter is that every single player on our roster was the best player on her club team, and on any given weekend, eight of those players don't even travel. What you did in high school or club doesn't matter anymore. If you want more playing time, then you'll just have to become a better player.

I've known a lot of coaches, both good and bad. Many have an amazing understanding of the game while others still have some work ahead of them. But I've never met a coach who didn't genuinely believe that he was putting his best line-up on the field. I've never once heard a coach say he was going to play a lesser player over a better player because he liked the lesser player more. It just doesn't happen. When it's game day, no one wants to win more than the coach. No coach is going to diminish his chances to win a game because he likes one kid more than another. Remember that. We might be dumb, but we're not *that* dumb.

I've been very fortunate to genuinely like almost every player I've ever coached. There have only been two or three players that I just couldn't stand. But you know what? Those two or three players helped my team win games, so they played. They started and they played because we were a better team with them on the field. As I mentioned earlier, sports are the ultimate meritocracy. The best players play, whether I like them or not. I don't have to like a player for her to get on the field. Remember that, too.

The surest way to earn more playing time is to become a better player. Coaches can help with that, but they don't wave magic wands. Improvement takes time, effort and lots of repetition. Don't underestimate the value of hard work and time spent with a ball. If your child isn't playing as much as you or she would like, maybe it's not because of the coach. You have to honestly consider the possibility that your daughter isn't playing as much as the other kids because the other kids are just better than she is. If that's the case, then your child has a choice to make. She can either choose to spend more time working on her skills away from the scheduled team practice sessions - while *also* supporting the team and the coach - or she can bite her tongue and look for a new team when the season ends. Those are the only two acceptable options.

When you equate playing time with happiness, you walk a slippery slope. Do you want the coach to make your kid happy by giving her more playing time? Well who doesn't? Every other parent wants the exact same thing, right? But it is literally impossible for the coach to please all of those parents; our math problem showed us that. If you are one of the parents who aren't pleased, your only choice is how you will respond to your adversity. I know it's difficult because you love your kid, but I beg of you, choose to handle your suffering with dignity and honor. Take the high road. Don't become a cancer to your team. Don't convince your daughter she's a victim, because that can become a very dangerous habit for her. Find a better way.

If you feel compelled to address playing time issues, let me suggest a wonderful approach. I would say that once the player hits the age of 13, this should come directly from the player to the coach without the involvement of a parent if at all possible. But ultimately that's going to be your call. Regardless, try phrasing your query like this: *"Coach, in what areas do I need to improve so I have a chance to earn more playing time?"*

It's a perfectly reasonable question and phrased in a most diplomatic way. The player is putting the responsibility on herself to improve without turning blame on anyone else. The player is taking responsibility for her current predicament, and coaches appreciate that. The player is not looking for a gift; she is looking to *earn* those minutes. Most coaches will be happy to provide suggestions for improvement along with some training exercises that will help your daughter address those areas.

Asking your coach to identify areas for improvement is not where this one ends. That's just the first step. The real key is working to actually improve in those areas.

The very best players I've coached are starved for this type of feedback. They are constantly asking for new challenges. They'll turn a list of weaknesses into a to-do list and then go to work knocking them out. Let me give you an example.

A few years ago we had a player who we felt was talented enough to eventually represent the U.S. National Team. In addition to being exceptionally talented, she was always coming out to training sessions an hour early to work on some aspect of her game. She wanted to take any potential weakness in her game and not just correct it, but transform it into a legitimate strength. Her pursuit of excellence was truly remarkable and it was the major reason why she had become so talented in the first place.

I really wanted her to make a push for the national team because I believed she was capable of playing at that level, but I didn't want it to be my idea. For this grand initiative to have any merit, it had to come from her. But wouldn't you know, she never mentioned it.

So I waited. And waited. And I waited some more. It was frustrating because in my heart I knew this girl had the potential to play in a World Cup. I was stuck in a holding pattern, waiting for her to believe the same thing.

Months went by. Then a year. Then a year and a half. Then one Saturday, while I was out of town at a recruiting event, she sent me this text: *"I want to be on the national team."*

It was fantastic! It came from out of nowhere, but I was ecstatic nonetheless. It was the opening I had been waiting for! But I didn't want to sign on until I knew she was fully committed to reaching her goal, so I decided to challenge her. I wanted her to prove that she was serious about doing the work. So I responded: *"Can you juggle to 50 using only your left foot?"*

"Not yet."

"When you can juggle to 50 using only your left foot, then I'll get interested."

To put this challenge into perspective for you, I have never coached a player of either gender who could juggle to 50 using only his weak foot. I was a juggling junkie during my college days and had no problem juggling into the thousands, but if you asked me to juggle with only my left foot, I may have gotten to ten. You'll just have to believe me that this challenge is exceptionally difficult.

I figured she would conquer this challenge the same way she conquered all the other challenges I had ever given her. She would put her head down and grind it out until she had won. I expected that I would hear from her in a few days.

About two hours later she texted me again: *"87. What's next?"*

Wow! I had given her a challenge – a big one – just to see how serious she was. She threw on her shoes, grabbed a ball and went down to the local park and didn't stop until she had obliterated it. When your coach gives you an area for improvement, that's a pretty good idea of the response he's hoping you'll give him.

There are a few reasons I'm sharing that story with you. First of all, it's a good illustration of a player who was genuinely serious about improving. She wasn't looking for more playing time. As talented as she was, you have to remember that she was still just trying to make a team!

Some players feel that their playing time should automatically increase as a reward for putting in a few extra hours, but that's not how it works. Your playing time increases when your ability improves. If your child is going to put in the extra time, make sure she understands that; then give her some guidance about how to reach her goals.

I also gave you that story so you can pass it along to your own daughter because if she has visions of rising high up the pyramid, one day she may have to compete against the player I just told you about. Players with that type of dedication are out there, even if you can't see them. It's only fair that you let your daughter know who she's going to run up against one day. Right now she might be a big fish in a small pond, but at the top of the pyramid, that's where the man-eaters swim.

By the way, it's not the worst idea in the world for a player to periodically ask her coach to suggest areas for improvement, even if she is already playing every minute of every game. We're never too good to stop learning and improving.

When the issue is playing time, you have to first put the onus on your daughter so she has the chance to respond. Guide her into the honorable response of putting in a greater effort. Let her make the investment. Nothing worthwhile is easy, and that also applies to soccer.

Some parents bounce their kid from club to club looking for the coach who is smart enough to recognize the soccer genius that is their child. I advise you to avoid this. When you are bouncing your daughter from one club to the next, soccer has stopped being her thing and started being yours.

Before you decide on moving clubs, ask yourself this very simple question: *Would my daughter be playing more if she was a better player?* If the answer is yes, then the solution is relatively straightforward: Let her decide if she wants to put in the time and effort to become a better player. Before you start casting blame, give your daughter a chance to stand up and fight her own fight. Explain to her that right now, the coach feels that some other players are ahead of her and if she wants to eventually leapfrog those players, she may have to practice soccer on her own, outside of the weekly team sessions. If she jumps at the chance to practice more and follows through by actually spending time with the ball, then her chances of playing more minutes are going to improve dramatically. On the other hand, if putting in the extra time just isn't worth it to her, then you've got to wonder why her lack of playing time even bothers you.

20

Avoid Comparisons

An excellent way to guarantee that your child's coach will stop taking your calls is to compare your child to other players on the team. There is never a right time or place to say, *"Well, Billy is better than Peter, why isn't he playing in front of him?"*

When you start doing this, you are begging, and I mean *begging* for trouble. For starters, your coach never wants to hear from you again. Secondly, when word gets to Peter's family, which it most certainly will, well then you're going to have a whole new set of enemies. At that point you graduate from being a disgruntled parent to being a cancer.

Too many of us have seen relationships ruined because Billy's parents are unhappy and just can't stop themselves from badmouthing Peter. What you have to remember is that Peter doesn't decide who plays and for how long. Peter has no control over playing time. That is strictly a coach's decision. Make sure you're not making derogatory comments about a teammate simply for doing his best.

Never cast your child's teammate in a negative light. Think of this as more than just advice; take it as another *commandment*. Don't compare your child to one of his teammates; don't gossip or spread rumors about one of his teammates;

don't even concern yourself with his teammates in any negative way whatsoever. If you do, yes, you're going to get some fallout, but your child will end up buried beneath the rubble. Your trespasses will follow him from soccer to school to everywhere else. Don't let soccer turn you into a monster. Don't let it ruin your relationships or your child's relationships. Take the high road as a good and decent human being. You won't regret it.

21

Show Up To
The Games

Kids love it when their parents watch them play (as long as sideline etiquette is adhered to) and your coach knows that. Because it means a lot to your child, it means a lot to your coach. Your child wants you to watch him because he's been working really hard to improve and he wants you to be proud of him. He wants you to see him doing something that he loves doing. Take an active interest in soccer because to your child, it's more than just a hobby. The more supportive you are of your son's soccer experience, the more likely he is to stay involved.

22

Stay Off The Field

Somewhere along the way your little Billy is going to take a ball to the face or a cleat to the toe or a boot to the shin. It's soccer. These things happen. When they do, and little Billy is rolling around holding his face/toe/shin and tears are streaming down his face, your maternal or paternal instincts are going to tell you to run onto the field and tend to your son. Please don't.

First of all, it's not your job. Secondly, unless you've got some advanced medical training, you're not going to do any good anyway. When Billy hits the turf, don't panic. Stay calm. Stand on the sidelines looking worried and biting your nails if you must, but don't go running onto the field.

There are almost no fatal soccer injuries, so it's not like you need to rush out there to say your last goodbyes. Give the coaching staff some space and a chance to do their job. When the coach or trainer is concentrating on repairing your son, the last thing he needs is you getting in the way. If the injury is serious enough, the coach may eventually wave you onto the field. At that point you are welcome to go out there and console your son.

Assuming the injury is not of the life-threatening nature, let me give you a really great reason not to come running onto the field, and it has to do with your child's development as a person and a player. If your child is 12 or younger, you really need to pay attention here. The younger your child, the more closely you need to follow along.

When you run out to tend to Billy's limp and lifeless body, do you know what the first words out of your mouth are going to be? I do. You're going to say, *"Are you okay?"*

I've coached thousands of kids during soccer camps, so I've seen my share of 'injuries'. I've been the first responder to a great many of them. Do you know what my experience has taught me? The *extent* of the injury (and thus the child's response) is directly proportional to the reaction of the first responder. It's amazing, but often times the child determines his action based on the first adult to reach him. If the first responder has pity in his voice and says, *"Awww, are you okay?"* I guarantee you that as sure as the sun rises and sets, that kid is going to start bawling his eyes out. But, if the first responder says, *"Wow! That was awesome! You are so brave! Man I love how brave you are,"* that kid is going to stand up and shake it off and carry on with the game. You may think I'm nuts, but I've been using this approach for two decades and the success rate is astronomical! It works because often times the player is more scared than he is hurt, and when you rave about how brave he is in front of 20 of his peers, he will do everything in his power to prove you right! Does it always work? No. But if it doesn't work, it's usually because the kid really is still feeling a significant amount of pain.

Pain tolerance is a part of growing up and we have more control over it than you might realize. When it comes to physical pain, we can actually choose not to cry. Give your child a chance to respond to physical pain. Resilience is an important survival skill.

When your son or daughter ends up on the ground after a collision, don't be a drama queen and rush the field clutching your rosary and yelling, *"Call 9-1-1!"* All you're going to do is ensure that your child will end up on the ground more often and for longer periods of time and that the other parents are going to start referring to you as the whacko. There is something a little bit heroic about being injured in the name of competition. When it happens, it is your kid's moment. Don't steal his thunder. Let him stay down on the ground collecting himself, clicking his bones back in their proper places. Let the drama build. When he finally stands and shakes out the cobwebs, everyone will applaud and life as you know it will resume. He'll rise up like a conquering hero feeling the adoration of the masses as they applaud his courage to press on.

Note: If you recognize an injury that is obviously life threatening to any player — like a seizure or a serious head trauma — and you are qualified and certified to help, then by all means, don't wait. Get out on the field and do your thing.

Finally, I hope it goes without saying that you should also never enter the field of play to confront any player, coach or official.

23

Stay Away From The Bench

When the game is in progress or about to start, stay away from the team bench. Don't stop by to say hi to your daughter or to give her a last minute pep talk or remind her where you are going after the game. Figure this stuff out before she gets out of the car.

The bench area is sacred territory to a coach and a team. When a player gets to that bench, she should be switched on and focused on the game at hand. Breeching that area is incredibly disrespectful to your coach. We take these things seriously. I'm not kidding.

If you visit the bench, you are a distraction at best, so please don't do it. Don't go over there. Just stay away. And seriously, is there anything you're going to say that can't wait until after the game?

Remember, you have to release your child and that means knowing your boundaries. Parents who pop by the bench are a special kind of annoying for coaches.

24

Common
Courtesy And The
Commitment

In this age of rush, rush, rush and go, go, go, there's a simple premise that a parent can easily lose sight of, but remembering it will do a world of good for your relationship with the coach: *Your time isn't any more valuable to you than your coach's time is to him.* I cannot possibly overstate this. It doesn't matter how much you love your kid or how much money you make or what your social standing is in the community, your time isn't any more valuable to you than your coach's time is to him. Please try to remember that.

When the coach is running practice, he's actually busy. This isn't the time to walk up and discuss whatever happens to be on your mind. I know you want to talk because you'll be busy later, but he's busy now. Talk to the coach before practice starts or after it ends. Yes, it will cost you an extra five minutes, but side-stepping that perceived disrespect will be well worth it in the long run.

Get your child to practice on time. When you are habitually late, you are telling the coach that you don't respect what she's doing. The coach may smile and wave at you anyway, but in her mind she's thinking, *'Well, thank you for gracing us with your presence. I hope we haven't been too much of an inconvenience.'*

This can be a really difficult situation for parents to make peace with because you've got a lot of real world issues to handle outside of soccer. Your coach understands that, but you need to understand that your coach walks a fine line. What might not seem like a big deal to you can be a very big deal to some other people. Remember, as we learned earlier, coaches have to be extremely careful about setting bad precedents.

Coaching is a juggling act on a high wire. You're constantly trying to balance what is right with what is fair with what will be in the team's best interest with what will help you win the next game and doing all of these things under a microscope. And of all the balls your coach is keeping in the air, none is more precarious than the one labeled *playing time.* Your coach knows that playing time is the currency of youth soccer for players and their parents.

When your kid is late, it puts the coach in a very awkward position, because now he's got some difficult decisions to make. If Sally is competing for a starting spot with your daughter Jenny, and Sally got to practice on time but Jenny was late, do you think it's fair to give Jenny the starting spot in the next game? Would you expect the coach to reward Jenny for being late?

A lot of parents try to jump on the grenade when it comes to tardiness because they provide their child's transportation. Let's clear this one up right now. Just because you are the one driving the car, it doesn't mean that your daughter is exempt from the repercussions. Saying, *"It wasn't Jenny's fault; it was mine"*, just doesn't cut it because it doesn't make Sally and her parents any less irritable and it doesn't get the coach off the hook. Believe me when I tell you that disgruntled parents are always looking for reasons to shoot the coach, and we don't like it when you hand them the ammunition. You can't put the coach in a difficult spot and then expect to enjoy the results. If you are responsible for your child's transportation, then in that setting, you are an extension of your child. If you're late, then your kid is late and that's just how it goes.

Your player is a part of something bigger. Her teammates and coaches are counting on her. She is accountable to a force much bigger than herself. Being late is not only disrespectful to the coach; it's disrespectful to the entire team.

Coaches know how important it is to get started on time, that's why they are so fond of saying, *"On time means early."* Coaches have a plan in place and executing that plan requires adhering to a pretty tight timeline. Players who show up late unbalance the whole load.

A big slice of the coaching pie is dedicated to planning – planning practices and starting line-ups and substitution patterns and team functions. It is important that a coach knows how many players she has available on any given day. There are many training exercises that you can run with 12 players but not with 11, or with 16 players but not 15. When a coach draws up her practice plan, her selection of exercises is predicated on the number of players she is expecting at training. All it takes is one missing cog to flummox the whole machine.

Incidentally, if you are guilty of this infraction and still want to earn a gold star, be a hero by stepping up and taking responsibility. Tell the coach it was your fault, you're sorry, it won't happen again, and you completely understand if Jenny doesn't get to start in the next game. Jenny might not be thrilled with that approach, but it's a great way to slip a valuable life lesson her way.

Of course, sometimes life will just reach up and bite you in the butt and you're going to have to deal with an unforeseen emergency. Coaches understand that. We know that there are certain things in life that must take priority over soccer. When one of these moments pops up and you are going to be either late or absent, all we ask is that you let us know with as much advance notice as possible. In this day and age, there is no excuse for not getting the message to your coach. Cell phones have made all of us very accessible and coaches are no exception. When you fail to make these calls, what you're really saying is that you don't value your coach's time or her work. Your coach might not be happy that Jenny can't make it to practice, but she'll appreciate the fact that you showed the common decency to give her the chance to rework her plan.

Being on time also applies to the end of practice and is also a part of your commitment. If you're a parent who drops your son off for the start of practice, make sure you are physically there to retrieve him when practice ends. When the coach is ready to leave the field and move on to the next thing in his life, he doesn't want to have to wait around for Billy's mom to show up. At that point he has transitioned from coach to babysitter and I guarantee you he's not the least bit happy about it. Coaches sign up to coach, not to be an extension of your daycare. It is horribly unfair to leave the coach in charge of your child so you can finish up your errands. How would you feel if you suddenly had to stay late at the office to babysit the boss' kid? What if you had big plans for that night? I assure you that the irritation you think you might feel is significantly less than the irritation you would actually feel.

Tardiness and absenteeism are behaviors sure to aggravate your coach because they indicate a lack of courtesy and a lack of commitment. Make no mistake about it; coaches are big on commitment and they have a right to be, because they make a big commitment themselves.

For your coach, soccer functions are not optional. And guess what, they aren't optional for your child either. When you sign your son or daughter up to be a part of a team, you are making a commitment for your child to attend all of that team's games and practices and other activities. When you start trivializing soccer as an optional activity to occupy some of your son's free time, you are missing the target by a country mile.

There's a difference between signing up for a soccer team and signing up for an activity like a spin class, even though you may pay the same amount of money for both. The spin class is an individual activity that happens to involve a collection of people gathering at the same time. It doesn't matter whether or not you happen to show up. If you miss your spin class, it has no significant effect on the other participants. They're going to jump on their stationary bicycles and pedal away just like they do every other time the class meets. One person's absence doesn't affect the performance of the whole group in the present or future. A soccer team has an entirely different dynamic and regardless of how much money you pay, you are still expected to honor the commitment you made by signing up. Paying doesn't make it optional.

A soccer team isn't just a collection of players; it's a process, and that process never truly ends. There is always room for improvement and that improvement hinges on the ability of the players to work together. That ability relies on players showing up and developing a greater understanding of their roles. So yes, it does matter that you get your kid to every practice and every game, even on the days when you'd rather not.

The coach can't just pick the days he wants to show up and then bail on the others. He can't just pick the days when he will show up on time. He has a commitment to every player and every parent on the team. If he starts flaking out on those commitments, you're going to be a very unhappy parent. And that's exactly how he feels about the attendance habits of his players. Just because there are many players, that doesn't dilute the responsibility of each player to honor his commitment. You can't hide behind all of the other drops in the bucket. Don't exist believing that it really doesn't matter if your one child doesn't show up this one time. It does matter. To your coach it matters a lot!

Yes, I understand that surprises happen, but remember, you've made a commitment to your team. Once you've made that commitment, you don't get to make other commitments that will preempt your current one. By definition, making a commitment means saying no to things that will conflict with that commitment. It means saying no to some other opportunities that may arise. Your son might have to miss a friend's birthday party or an invitation to your neighbor's lake house. It doesn't matter how great the new opportunity is, you've got to say no. That's what it means to make a commitment.

I think that most coaches end up coaching because they loved being a part of a team at least as much as they loved playing the sport. When you grow up under the umbrella of a team, you internalize intangibles such as accountability and commitment and loyalty and teamwork, and you come to understand the immense and beautiful power of a group of people who are all truly committed to a common cause and to looking out for one another. The values you develop within the team experience become second nature. You understand how much better life is with the power of a team behind you and you want other people to get that same experience and it can be absolutely maddening when those people can't seem to stop dipping their toes in the water and jump in the darn pool!

I genuinely feel a little bit sorry for the people who have never had the experience of being fully involved in a team sport. In many ways, when it comes to the concepts of 'team' and 'commitment,' they just don't get it. They don't know what it means to take the field with a collection of brothers to fight the good fight against an opponent who is clearly superior. They don't understand the bonds that are formed under the shared misery of an unholy fitness session or a four-hour stay on the side of the interstate when the bus breaks down. They can't understand how someone can volunteer to make his own life more painful so his teammate's life can be a little less so. They've never had the friends who truly had their back when things got truly awful. These are some of the most treasured and memorable experiences of my life and I got to have all of them because I was lucky enough to be a teammate.

When you treat soccer like an activity class, you're cheating your child out of the best part of team sports. He's never going to know what it's like to have teammates committed to him until he is a committed teammate himself. The shared commitment is what separates soccer from spinning. Showing up and being on time are more than just a matter of politeness; they are excellent life policies that gather excellent life experiences. To get the best out of soccer, you have to commit to it, even on the days when you might wish you hadn't. On days when soccer may seem like an inconvenience, you've got to make an attempt to see the bigger picture. You've got to trust that soccer is going to provide a much bigger experience than what you see running around out there on the field.

25

Believe Your Coach

If your daughter's coach told you that she was really improving on her dribbling and shooting and turning into quite a talented soccer player, would you believe him? Of course you would! Why on earth wouldn't you believe him? That's great news!

Well, what you have to remember is that the news isn't always going to be great. But that won't make it any less truthful. One of the grand surprises of my coaching experience has been those moments when a parent just flat out didn't believe me.

I was speaking with a high school teacher who told me about an incident she recently had with a female student and her parent. The teacher had caught the girl cheating on an exam. This is obviously a big deal and the girl was facing serious disciplinary action. The girl's mother came down to meet with the teacher about what had happened. The teacher explained how the student had been caught copying answers from another student and how she was now facing suspension and possible expulsion.

The mother turned to her daughter and asked, *"Is this true?"*

With one simple question the mother implied that the teacher might be lying. The daughter saw the narrow window of escape and jumped for it. *"No,"* she said.

The mother mulled it over for a moment, then turned to the teacher and flatly said, *"She didn't do it."*

The mother, who was not in that classroom and who had not seen what the teacher had, decided that her child could not possibly have cheated on that exam. Why? Because *my daughter wouldn't do that!*

Can you imagine the teacher's frustration? In that moment, in spite of doing her job to the best of her ability in a very difficult situation, the mother was calling the teacher a liar.

All parents would be better served if we took a moment to accept the fact that our kids are not angels. They make mistakes. They test their boundaries. They experiment. They lie. They do whatever they think they need to do to serve their own best interests at any given moment. Do you know why they do these things? Because they are human and humans are nothing if not imperfect. Don't kid yourself into believing that your child doesn't lie. I coach your kids when they get to college and they lie to me all the time. And you'd be stunned to know how often they lie to you, too.

If I surveyed the parents of 1000 random high school seniors and asked them if their child ever used marijuana, how many affirmative responses do you think I would get? Five? Ten? Fifty? I'd be amazed if 50 parents would answer yes to that question. I'd be amazed if 50 parents had that much of a grip on what behaviors their children are actually engaging in. But you know what? We'd still be way off the mark because statistics from the National Institute on Drug Abuse tell us that of those 1000 high school seniors, 214 of them smoked marijuana *in the past 30 days!* Do you honestly think that there's no way on earth that your children might be keeping some secrets from you? Of course they are! That's what kids do! They know that there are certain behaviors that you've deemed unacceptable and engaging in those behaviors will result in some serious consequences. Kids are going to experiment with some of those behaviors and then do whatever is necessary to avoid those consequences. So they do what kids do… They lie. Yes, even to you.

Do you remember that really famous murder trial where the prosecution presented its evidence and then the judge found the defendant guilty before the defense team ever got to present its case? Of course you don't, because it never happened. There are two sides to every story and that little truism makes up the foundation of our entire jurisprudence system. Try to keep that in mind when your child comes home from soccer in a foul mood because of something the coach did or said. Remember that you are only getting half the story, and it's always the half that favors your kid.

Years ago I was coaching a day camp for boys between the ages of 9-11. We finished each afternoon with a small-sided scrimmage. During one of these scrimmages, a boy I'll call Mike tripped another boy from behind. I called the foul and warned Mike that what he had done was unacceptable. A few minutes later, Mike did the same thing to the same boy. Again I called the foul and warned him; this time with a bit more enthusiasm. Sure enough, a few minutes later, Mike whacked the legs out from this boy for the third time, and this foul was the worst of the bunch. I mean Mike absolutely swatted him.

Now I was upset. I had been playing and coaching soccer long enough to know what fouls are inadvertent and what fouls are intentional, and this third foul was certainly intentional. There were only ten minutes left in the camp day, so I pulled Mike off the field and told him he wasn't allowed to play anymore that day. As I was scolding him, one of the things I said was, *"You're lucky that boy didn't get up and punch you."*

Even as the words were leaving my mouth I was trying to pull them back in, but alas, no such luck. Ah yes, from the category of verbiage I wish I could take back.

The next morning the boy's father was there to confront me. Why? Because I was being unfair to his son and because *I threatened to punch the boy.*

Huh?

That's right. That's the story the boy had told his father. The boy had gotten home that day, looked his father in the eye and lied through his teeth. And the father bought every word of it. He actually believed I had threatened to punch his eleven-year-old son. You can imagine the mood he was in when he showed up that morning.

I quickly explained that the story he had heard was fictional and then led him through what had actually transpired, step by step. I explained the three fouls. I explained that we were lucky the other boy hadn't gotten hurt. And I explained what I actually said.

The father must have had some nagging suspicions about the boy's story in the first place as he quickly abandoned the notion that I threatened to punch his son. Strangely enough, what he couldn't square with was the fact that I had judged his son to have committed an intentional foul. He said, *"Well I know my son, and he isn't that type of player."*

"Okay, I can agree to that if you can agree that I've been playing and coaching soccer for over 20 years and that I have a pretty good grasp of the game and that of the two of us, I was the only one who was actually here yesterday."

It didn't matter. Logic wasn't going to win the day. The dad was sticking by his son and removed him from the camp. If you think an incident like this doesn't stick with a coach, consider that I am writing about it nearly 15 years after it happened.

Eventually your child will grow up and get a driver's license. Then one day he's going to come home, shaking in his shoes as he tells you he got a speeding ticket. And guess what – you're not going to be mad at the cop. But you are going to be mad as heck at your son for driving irresponsibly and costing you $135 that you weren't planning on spending. You're not going to reflexively think that the cop had to be wrong because your son would never speed! You're going to assume that the cop got it right. Why? Because you're not completely insane!

I wasn't out to get that boy at camp, and your daughter's coach isn't out to get her either. In our culture, teachers and coaches are called on to serve as a loosely assembled police force. They set rules and administer consequences when those rules are broken. It's the only way it can work.

You can't go through life thinking that your kid will never break a rule. You can't assume that the coach got it wrong just because you didn't like how it turned out. You have to understand that your coach isn't out to get your kid.

If the coach tells you that Susie won't be starting on Saturday because she back-talked or because she was verbally abusive to a teammate, then you can bet your backside that's exactly what happened.

You see your child through rose-colored glasses and that's all good and well, but you've got to get realistic every now and then. Eventually you just have to believe your coach, even when the news is bad. This also applies to the feedback your coach offers from a purely soccer standpoint.

Many soccer players, and their parents, are starved for feedback. Don't confuse feedback with effusive praise. Feedback is an objective evaluation of your son's performance, both good and bad. I recommend that you pay attention to the positive *and* negative elements of these evaluations. As I mentioned earlier, the best players I've coached were starved for feedback, particularly about their weaknesses.

Coaches critique players because that's their job. They don't do it to hurt your son's feelings. When a coach offers a suggestion for improvement, he's actually trying to help your son improve as a soccer player, not criticize your son as a person. Understand the difference and encourage your child to do the same. Feedback is a valuable commodity. When your coach offers up some feedback, consider it a favor and use it to your advantage.

26

Button The Loose Lips

Before you vent your frustration, *think*! Ask yourself if what you are about to say is going to undermine the coach. If you think that's even a possibility, then swallow it. Once your kid hears it, there's no taking it back. It might make you feel better in the moment, but the damage you will cause just isn't worth it.

You are a traffic light for what is acceptable and unacceptable behavior for your child. If you express it, that gives your child a green light to express it also. Saying something as simple as, *"I don't know why he didn't let you take that free kick,"* gives your child a green light to outwardly question the coach's decisions. When that happens, you've started a small snowball rolling down the mountain that's eventually going to become the giant snowball that runs over the cabin that sits down in the valley.

For your team to reach its potential, the players have to trust the coach, and that means you agree to trust him also. Now you only have to make that agreement one season at a time, but that's the social contract you enter into when you join a team. You agree to trust and support that coach from beginning to end and to accept his decisions, even the ones you don't agree with. If you can't bring yourself to outwardly support him, then just take the high road and button your lip. Then when the season ends, if you're still unsatisfied with the coach's performance, join a new team.

27

The Squeaky Wheel

Perhaps the greatest frustration coaches face is dealing with entitlement issues from players and their parents. Everybody wants what they want and they want it now; and once they have it, they want more. The reserve player just wants to play. She swears up and down that's all she wants. She just wants to get on the field so she can truly feel like a part of the team. Then once she's playing on a regular basis, she's unhappy because she's not a starter. Then she becomes a starter but she's unhappy because she wasn't named as a captain. Meanwhile, a year earlier, all she wanted was to play.

Unfortunately, entitlement is a battle coaches face regularly because entitlement is a part of human nature. Give us an inch and we want a mile. And I'm no different.

I spent 23 years of my adult life being single. Every morning for 23 years I would wake up, head straight to the kitchen and make myself a pot of coffee. Then I got married and my wonderful wife, Beth, brought an automatic coffee-maker into my life. That coffee-maker worked on a timer. Each night before she went to bed, Beth would set up the coffee and program the timer so the pot would start brewing just before I woke up. Each and every morning for six weeks I woke up to a pot of hot, fresh, delicious coffee. It was fantastic!

And then one day it wasn't.

One morning I woke up and went out to the kitchen where I discovered a tremendous injustice: There was no coffee brewing! Beth had forgotten to set the timer! Unthinkable! And guess what... I was bitter! How could *she* forget my coffee!

Yes, I'm horribly embarrassed that my reflex reaction was bitterness. But that's how human nature works. Instead of being thankful that I hadn't had to make my own coffee for six weeks, I was annoyed that my wife had forgotten to make it for me on this one morning. I was actually irritated that I would have to do exactly what I had done for the previous 23 years: make my own coffee. Somehow, after six short weeks, I felt entitled to having coffee magically appear for me each morning. Why? Because that's exactly the way the world is supposed to cater to me!

Thankfully it only took about three seconds to get my head right and put things back into perspective. Unfortunately, some people never find that perspective and as a result we've developed a generation of kids (and parents) who float through life feeling that the world owes them something. And a whole lot of them play soccer.

This culture of entitlement that now pervades us has been accelerated by this notion that the squeaky wheel gets the oil. Somehow we've come to believe that if we complain enough about anything, someone will feel obliged to bend over backwards to erase the unpleasantness that has besieged us. There may be a time and place for that, but your child's soccer team provides neither.

Before you choose to position yourself as the squeaky wheel, hit the brakes and find some perspective. Before focusing squarely on where your child is, take a moment to reflect on where she's been. Too many people focus on what they don't have and forget about all they actually do have. When the spirit urges you to vent, it may be worth taking a moment to catalogue all of the positive things that soccer is providing for your child.

I'm not saying that your child shouldn't have higher goals for herself. She should! I'm just saying that the proper way to reach those goals is through good, old-fashioned, hard work; not whining until she gets her way.

It's worth repeating: sports are a meritocracy. The best rise to the top. There are no shortcuts, no matter how badly you wish there were. Remind yourself of that before the cloud of entitlement starts to fog your brain. The soccer experience can be a wonderful ally in your child's overall development. Don't treat it like a plate of nuggets that came out cold. It deserves more consideration than that.

If you plan on operating under the philosophy that the squeaky wheel gets the oil, I feel obliged to remind you of the coaches' response: *The squeaky wheel is also the one that gets replaced.*

28

Let Your Child Speak

As I was deciding whether or not to write this segment, I got an email which confirmed that including it was a good idea. The email was from the father of a high school sophomore telling me his daughter is a gifted soccer player and citing the various awards she has won and how she wants to play college soccer for us. And oh yeah, she would also like a scholarship. I get a few of these emails each year and I delete them all. Let me explain why.

College coaches have to decide if they want to adopt your daughter for four years. When a prospect won't stand on her own two feet and speak for herself, we see a great big, red flag. By her sophomore year of high school, there are certain areas where your daughter needs to be able to stand tall and make a case on her own behalf. Pretty much anything that relates to sports would qualify as one of those areas.

Don't get me wrong; we certainly want to develop a relationship with the parents and involve them in the recruiting process, but not before we've been introduced to the player. A soccer game is a collection of individual battles. It takes a degree of physical, mental and emotional strength to win them. A player who can't write her own email or make her own phone call seems like someone who is going to need a whole lot of handholding. That type of girl screams of timidity. We don't want timid. We want warriors. If your daughter is too shy to call me, I question her ability to help us win championships.

Soccer can be a wonderful aid to your child's development into a productive, functional adult – *if* you let it. You can't always jump in front of your child to make her case; nor should you. You're not going to be able to fight all of her battles for her. You won't be in the room when she has that big job interview, and you won't be the one asking her boss for a raise. If you never let her fight her own battles, she'll never develop the capacity to win them. Soccer provides an excellent testing ground for mild confrontation, and that's going to help her out somewhere down the road. At a certain age, your daughter needs to speak on her own behalf.

Coaches appreciate the players who address them directly if for no other reason than it gives the coach a chance to solve a problem he might have never knew existed. Problems tend to get magnified when parents become involved. Before a mole hill becomes a mountain, encourage your daughter to address the coach directly. The solution might be fairly simple. That's not always the case, but sometimes we get lucky.

If your teenager feels she isn't being treated fairly in terms of playing time, it's her issue to solve. Instead of morphing into your daughter's campaign manager and rushing to her rescue, why not encourage her to address the problem like a responsible young adult? You can sure as heck offer her some pointers of what to say and how to say it, but put the responsibility on your teenager to start solving her own problems, because one day she's going to be all grown up and this type of experience will come in handy.

29

Respect Boundaries

Non-coaches tend to think that soccer is all that coaches want to think about. That isn't quite true. Remember, your coach has a life outside of soccer. He may have a family or friends or hobbies that don't involve a ball and chances are that he doesn't want soccer bleeding over into those other areas.

When you get home from the office in the afternoon, do you want to spend the next five hours talking about work? Of course not. Neither does your coach. Soccer is already monopolizing a big chunk of his time and energy. When he gets the chance to break away, don't take it from him.

The bank won't take your call at 10 o'clock on a Sunday night; you shouldn't expect your coach to either. If you run into your coach at a restaurant having dinner with a special friend, don't feel obliged to wander over to his table and start talking about tryouts next month. A neighborly wave will suffice nicely.

Just remember that 'Coach' is the title, not the person, and give the guy some space. He'll appreciate that.

30

Solve Some Problems

Coaches love their low-maintenance families more than you can possibly imagine. Avoid asking your coach to solve problems that you are perfectly capable of solving yourself. Don't call your coach and ask him to find a store that sells cleats in Tommy's size. Don't ask him to find out if there will be a gluten-free option at soccer camp. If your soccer complex has a weather hotline and you need to find out if the fields are open or if your game has been cancelled, don't call the coach; call the hotline. Your soccer coach is there to coach soccer, not to be your valet. Solve these problems for yourself. Your coach has a real soft spot for low-maintenance families.

31

The Injury Conundrum

When I asked youth coaches for topics to include in this book, I was surprised that so many mentioned the expectations of playing time from a player who has been sidelined with an injury for any extended period. There's no single, magic-bullet solution for this one. Each coach will have his own policy for a player working his way back into the line-up, but more often than not, it's going to be handled on a case-by-case basis that will be heavily influenced by a host of external circumstances. However, regardless of your son's soccer prowess, if he's been missing training sessions due to an injury or illness, you should probably expect that he won't be in the starting line-up immediately upon his return. Why? Because that's just how it goes. You can also expect that when the Johnson boy gets back from his bout of mononucleosis, he will in fact immediately rejoin the starting line-up. Why? Because that's just how that one goes.

Coaches are always trying to walk the fairness high-wire and there's not much wiggle room up there. When a player comes back from an extended absence, the coach has a lot to think about, and believe me, he's thinking hard.

He's calculating a myriad of factors into his final decision and he knows that regardless of what he decides, someone is going to end up unhappy about it. That's just how it goes for him. You may be happy with his decision and if you are, I assure you that some other parent is not.

Let me give you some pointers on this one. First of all, if your son's extended absence is the result of your family's annual trip to Cabo, expect him to spend some time on the bench. If this seems unfair, please re-read the section on commitment.

If your son is bedridden with illness, there's not much you can do except feed him some chicken noodle soup and wait it out. But if he's out with an injury, I highly recommend that he continues to attend training sessions even though he isn't cleared to play and even if the coach doesn't require his attendance and even if the weather is miserable. Especially if the weather is miserable! Your boy can still find ways to contribute even if it's just by limping around and picking up cones. The simple act of showing up will underscore his commitment to the team and that will go a long way with his coach and teammates. And, from the standpoint of office politics, his attendance gives the coach some political cover. If the coach decides your son will start in the next game, no one can complain that it's not fair because your son wasn't at practice. Okay, he didn't do much at practice, but he was still there, and that's going to count for something.

If your son is suffering from an injury that prohibits him from participating with his team, his coach and teammates expect him to behave in a way that is conducive to his speedy recovery. If his ankle hurts too much to play soccer, no one will be very sympathetic if they see him at the skating rink on Friday night. Part of your son's commitment is to heal as quickly as possible so he can rejoin his team.

32

Help

Volunteers are the lifeblood of youth sports. When it's time for the car wash or the bake sale or the community service event or the end-of-season banquet, take a day out of your life and help out. Yeah, we all have places we'd rather be, but that's life. Suck it up and jump on board. Besides, these things usually turn out to be a lot of fun. If nothing else, it's an excellent way to make a deposit into your good karma account.

33

Be Responsible

Pay your dues on time; much like your electric bill, they aren't optional. Submit your paperwork on time. A coach or manager shouldn't have to spend her day chasing you around for these things. Send your kid to practice prepared. Make sure she's wearing the appropriate gear and that she brings her ball and that *her ball has air in it!* And when it's your turn to bring the snacks, please, bring the snacks.

34

Get Educated

Many leagues and clubs offer educational opportunities for parents with a wide array of topics ranging from Basic First Aid to the College Recruiting Process. They make these offerings for your benefit, so take advantage of them. Knowledge really is power.

35

If All Else Fails...

Remember the phrase commonly attributed to the Hippocratic Oath: *First do no harm*. That's an excellent jumping off point. If you want to have a positive relationship with your coach, first do no harm. Do not disqualify yourself by engaging in conduct detrimental to the team, its players or the coach. In other words, less is more.

36

Say Thank You

Every collegiate athletic department has at least one eligibility officer on staff. These are the people who make sure that players and recruits will be eligible to compete. I've had the opportunity to work with many fantastic eligibility officers. They've all been genuinely good people - some became great friends - and I've enjoyed seeing them outside of the office. However, anytime an eligibility officer unexpectedly shows up at my office, I cringe. It doesn't matter what he or she is wearing, all I see is a black, hooded cape and a sickle. Eligibility officers never just drop by to spread joy. If an eligibility officer appears on my doorstep, I'm expecting bad news. Youth soccer coaches may feel the same way when your name pops up on the caller ID. Chances are you're not calling them to express your merriment at the job they're doing. Very rarely does someone call the coach to offer good news or a pat on the back.

If you've ever worked in the food service industry, you know that waiters and bartenders are the world's best tippers. Why? Because they sympathize with you. They know the day you're probably having. They know the assembly line of joyless people who've brought their personal misery into your life. They know that you've bent over backwards catering to customers who've shown up with a laundry list of ways to make your job more difficult and then went light on the tip. In short, they feel your pain. The big tip they leave is their way of making sure you see some type of appreciation for a long shift of working a job that can strangle your morale. It's the best way they know to say thank you. And regardless of the job you do, everyone would like to feel at least a little bit appreciated for doing it to the best of their ability. That includes your coach. Two simple words will go a long way.

Honestly, all a coach would really like is to feel that her work, even the stuff you didn't see, hasn't gone unnoticed. If you want an easy way to forge a great relationship with your coach, start with a sincere thank you every now and then. Tell her thanks for being a good role model for your daughter, and for always doing her best, and for keeping your kid safe, and for valuing your child as more than just a soccer player. I cannot possibly overstate how far a genuine, heartfelt thank you will go. It's the best possible tip you can leave for your coach.

37

Some Parting Thoughts

I had no coaching aspirations when I finished college. I fell into it out of desperation. I was living in a Pittsburgh slum, flat broke and hungry when the opportunity to become a college coach presented itself, so I jumped at it. It was the happiest of accidents because, let's face it, even if coaching wasn't what I had intended on doing, I was in fact the perfect person to coach women's college soccer. Of course I was.

I knew my stuff, and man, wouldn't I just be the most inspiring coach these girls ever knew? I was going to change their lives! I was going to show them what a great soccer coach really was! I was going to be the guy who believed in them and who would lead them to amazing, new heights with nothing more than my sheer force of will. We were going to work hard together and it would be one-for-all and all-for-one and we were going to win more games than they had ever imagined possible, all because I was there now. I would be the coach they'd always dreamed of having; the inspirational force they had only encountered in Hollywood movies. They would hang on my every word. They would follow my every direction because I was just that fantastic! They would believe in me because they knew I would lead them to championships and that was all that mattered to college soccer players. We were going to win and everyone would be happy and I would be the reason for all of it! Yay me!

It took about a day and a half for me to wake up and realize that my grand vision of coaching was a far cry from the actual job. For starters, as a college soccer player, I genuinely thought that coaches sat around all day drawing up training sessions and then implementing them each afternoon. I thought that coaching was mostly about Xs and Os. Yeah. Fat chance.

I also assumed that as long as the team was winning, everyone would be happy. I reiterate, fat chance.

I assumed every player would love me. Ummm… notsomuch.

It didn't take long for reality to blow buckshot through my romanticized idea about the job of a coach. I had wholly underestimated the daily grind. Coaching isn't about Xs and Os, and win or lose, some people aren't going to be happy and not every player is going to love her coach and you're going to have some fantastic days and you're going to have some God-awful ones and you're going to be blamed for a lot of things that you really have no control over whatsoever and when you are being blamed, you'll often be the last one to know. In short, coaching ain't exactly what you see in the movies.

When people ask me about my job as a coach, I tell them that my average day is like your great day; my great days are indescribable; but my bad days, well, I wouldn't wish them on my worst enemy. And just so we're clear on this, my bad days have nothing to do with losing a soccer game.

Coaching is more about managing relationships than anything else. A coach wears many hats. At any given moment he will be called upon to be a parent, a teacher, a psychologist, a disciplinarian, a motivator, a babysitter, a cheerleader, a waiter, a butler, a fundraiser, a fortuneteller, a travel agent, a bodyguard and a politician. And occasionally, yes, he'll actually get to tinker with Xs and Os. The parent who understands that the coach's job goes far beyond the sport of soccer has a running start for building a mutually beneficial relationship.

I hope that this section has given you a broader understanding of the coach's role and provided you with the framework for developing a positive relationship with the guy who calls the shots. I hope it has given you some insight on the issues that your coach is dealing with on a daily basis. I wanted to shine a light on these things because too often we have a grand misconception about what coaching actually is. I hope I've shown you that coaching soccer is much, much more than designing drills for practice and picking a starting line-up. I hope you have a deeper insight into the multitude of factors a coach must consider when making decisions that would otherwise seem quite simple. And I hope that you will use this knowledge to forge a positive and productive relationship with your coach. If you do, you and your child will have a much more enjoyable experience.

When I polled coaches about this book and asked them what they would like the parents to know, this was one of the best responses I received. It comes from the coach of a high school girls' team.

Well first of all, I am human. Just like you, I have a conscience and I am constantly grading myself to see where I can become a better coach. I work really hard at making sure all of my girls know that they are important. I know the four years in high school are a very important time for your daughter and how she identifies herself amongst her peers. Trust me, I know this. I am in the business of building kids up, not tearing them down. However, for your daughter to grow, she has to go through some challenging times. Those will come in practices, games and video sessions. I have your daughter's best interest at heart. Remember, I WANT TO WIN. So please, don't approach me when you are mad without first thinking about the job I have to do, which is to win soccer games. I will not do that at the expense of your daughter's physical, mental or emotional well-being, so keep that in mind before approaching me.

The best parents I've had were the ones who gently ask, "Do you need anything?" Or, "Is there anything I can do for you?" That's what I need from you: support. I already put enough pressure on myself, so please, you don't need to add more onto that pile.

So there you have it. It doesn't take much to have a positive relationship with your coach. Just remember to first do no harm, and that when it comes to being a soccer parent, less is definitely more.

SECTION 3
WHAT THE REF
WANTS YOU
TO KNOW

38

The Men
(And Women)
In Black

Look, I really don't know why anyone in his right mind would want to get into the business of officiating soccer games, but sure enough, year after year a new batch of referees get their certifications and take their oaths and head out to soccer fields all across this great nation. God help them.

As you might expect, there is a healthy dropout rate amongst young soccer referees. I could tell you why, but I'm pretty sure you already know. Yep, *parents*. It doesn't take long for a referee to realize that the $30 he made for refereeing that U12 game was not worth the amount of verbal abuse he took from a sideline full of people who've never kicked a ball. In this case, the ref is Paul McCartney. You're still Yoko Ono.

I'll be the first to admit that there are good refs, bad refs, and good refs who have bad days. Regardless of the kind of day your official is having, if you have no soccer background, he still knows more than you. So before you decide to vent your frustration about the offside call the A.R. just missed, take a moment to understand why the referees are there in the first place. They are there to keep the game safe, to keep it flowing and to let the kids have fun. Don't just brush off that last sentence; think about it. Those things are really important.

Earlier I said that you are a stop light for your child and the behavior she will model regarding her coach. The same applies to your interactions with officials. Officials are authority figures, and your child will model her behavior after yours. Don't kid yourself that soccer games exist in some type of cosmic vacuum. You can't expect your child to compartmentalize soccer behavior away from the rest of life. If you think it's acceptable to berate an authority figure, your child will internalize that and store it in her subconscious and somewhere down the line it's going to come back to haunt both you and her. You are always a role model. You can be a good one or a bad one, but you are always a role model. Remember that.

I didn't write this book to advocate for referees. If I did, this chapter would be one sentence long: *Please don't yell at the officials.* I wrote the book to advocate for the 75% of our kids who quit by the age of 13. And part of the overall experience for those kids is the environment that surrounds their games. Your interaction with the officials is an undeniable part of that environment. Spectators can and often do set the tone for a match. Your behavior is contagious. Many otherwise restrained spectators have been goaded into saying *their piece* because someone else has shown no restraint in voicing his opinions to the referee. It's a behavior that will quickly snowball to the detriment of everyone involved in the game, including the players.

Officials understand that you are emotionally invested in the game, but before you feel obliged to voice your disapproval, here are some things they want you to know.

39

Officials Make Mistakes

Every official will admit that there are going to be some blown calls. Officials are human and they make mistakes, just like your daughter does when she's playing. If your daughter doesn't connect on a simple pass or mis-traps a ball or hits her shot over the goal, would you publicly berate her? Well I sure hope not! If we wouldn't berate our child for making a mistake, then why would we pounce on a referee for making one?

It can be a maddening experience when your officials are having a bad day. I totally get it. Believe me, I get it. But we're the grown-ups, so we've got to rise above our reflex reaction to vent whenever we perceive a miscarriage of justice. Before the game even begins, take a moment to remind yourself that the officials are going to make mistakes and that's just a part of this crazy, beautiful game we call soccer. Remind yourself that these guys are doing the best they can and that they aren't actually trying to make your team lose. If you do this before the game, you'll be much calmer during it, and that's good for everyone.

40

Offside Is Difficult

Offside may be the most difficult call in all of sports because there are so many moving pieces involved in making the call, and often times those pieces are separated by a good many yards. There is a level of precision involved in making this call that makes it far more difficult to judge than whether or not one player tripped another or committed a hand ball.

The key in judging whether or not a player is offside hinges on the very instant the ball was played. Let's face it, as spectators, we are watching the ball. After the ball gets played forward, that's when we turn our heads and make our judgment as to whether or not the attacker was offside. At that point, it's too late. If you are not looking across the field at the deepest defender at the precise instant the ball is struck, you really don't know if the attacker was onside or offside. That's precisely why the assistant referee keeps himself in line with the deepest defender. With all of soccer's moving pieces, when the ball leaves a player's foot, the A.R. has about one tenth of a second to evaluate the positioning of those pieces and make his decision. A tenth of a second! It takes a 90 m.p.h. fastball four times longer to reach home plate!

Do they always get it right? Of course not. But they get it right a lot more often than they get it wrong. I can't tell you the number of times I was absolutely convinced that an A.R. had blown an offside call, only to have video of the match prove that I was wrong and he was right. The A.R.s are in a much better position to make the call than you or I, so we may as well give them the benefit of the doubt.

41

It's Hard Enough To Be An A.R.

In a three-man officiating crew, the worst assignment is to be the assistant referee on the parents' sideline. For starters, the A.R. is the official responsible for calling offside, and that's difficult enough. Knowing that his every call is going to be met with a chorus of critiques from a sideline full of parents can be disheartening and distracting.

You want all of the officials to do the best possible job. That won't happen if the A.R. has to constantly contend with parents who want to debate him. Leave the guy alone and let him do his job.

And while we're at it, let me tell you a little secret: It's silly to argue about which team gets to take the throw-in. Why? *Because teams lose possession of their throw-ins about half of the time.* That means when your opponent is awarded a throw-in, there's an excellent chance that your team will end up with the ball. Why argue about it?

42

Learn The Rules

Some things in soccer that don't look like fouls actually are; and some things that look a lot like fouls actually aren't. The only way to know the difference is to understand the rules.

Recently I was watching a game at a recruiting showcase and saw one player absolutely bury another player. I mean she just lined the girl up and completely clobbered her! In that instant I was thinking, *What a great hit!* But before I could even finish my thought, I heard the chorus of protests from parents screaming, *"C'mon ref! Blow your whistle! That's horrible!"*

Look, just because your daughter got flattened, that doesn't automatically make it a foul. Soccer is a collision sport. That's why we play it on grass. Some days Susie is going to be the windshield; some days she's going to be the bug. It takes some training to know what qualifies as a foul and what does not.

You can't be a judge if you don't understand the law. And you shouldn't be a sideline ref if you don't know and understand the rules. Actually, you shouldn't be a sideline ref anyway, at least not a vocal one. But before you begin evaluating the officials' performance, you should probably have a pretty clear grasp of offside and advantage, and what qualifies as a direct or indirect free kick. If you want to learn the rules, start by purchasing a rule book. Just remember that soccer rules are being updated each year and do your best to stay informed of those changes.

Here is a link to the Soccer Association for Youth rules page: http://www.saysoccer.org/rulebook.aspx. It contains a helpful section that details the differences between its rules (some of which have been modified to accommodate various age groups) and FIFA rules.

Keep in mind that, particularly at the youngest age groups, the officials are learning to officiate, the same way your child is learning to play. If the officiating crew was amongst the world's best, they wouldn't be doing a U10 game. If all else fails and you think you can't stop yourself from unloading on that official, it will behoove you to remember that much like your son or daughter, that official is also somebody's child.

It's easy to vent your anger at the officials because they make really easy targets. But don't do it. Remember what's important. Hold yourself to a higher standard and focus on your job as a role model to your child.

If you want to go above and beyond the call of duty and really be a Gold Star Soccer Parent, then consider taking an officiating course. They are offered in every state. To learn how you can get started as a soccer official, visit this site: http://soccerrefereeusa.com. Heck, you may like it so much that you turn it into a part-time job. Then you can write your own book on why people shouldn't yell at the refs.

43

Remember The Message You're Sending

The comments you make to the officials during the game and what you say about them after the game will affect your child. Remember, you are a traffic light and your behaviors are constantly telling your child what is acceptable and what is not.

When you treat the officials with disrespect, you're giving your child the green light to disrespect future officials and other authority figures. This type of behavior can quickly parlay that $135 speeding ticket into handcuffs and a night in jail.

When you blame the referees for a result, or you entertain your child when he does that same thing, you are telling your son that he is a victim. This is an excellent way to end up with a whiny child who will never take responsibility for his own lot in life. There *should* be some adversity in our sporting endeavors. Our ability to overcome that adversity may be the single greatest satisfaction offered to us by sports. Instead of blaming the officials in a misguided effort to make yourself feel better, why not accept the fact that your team was beaten and ask your child to choose a better response?

I can't think of a better example of this in all of sports than the 2011 Women's World Cup quarter-final when the U.S. beat Brazil. Let's look at how officiating affected the circumstances.

With the U.S. leading 1-0, American Rachel Buehler was judged to have fouled a Brazilian player in the U.S. penalty box and Brazil was awarded a penalty kick. The call was questionable. The referee then compounded matters by ejecting Buehler from the contest. The U.S. would be forced to play the rest of the match 10 v 11 and everyone anticipated that Brazil would tie the game with the penalty kick. Remarkably, goalkeeper Hope Solo saved the penalty. However, with another bizarre judgment, the referee negated Solo's save for some phantom violation. An angry Solo was then issued a yellow card for protesting the decision and Brazil was allowed to retake the kick. On the ensuing shot, Brazil tied the game. So to summarize:

- *The initial penalty call was debatable*
- *The red card to Buehler was incredibly harsh*
- *The saved penalty was negated by a horrendous decision*
- *Solo was given a yellow card*
- *Brazil tied the game and would play the remainder of the match with a one-player advantage.*

Talk about a game-changing moment! If this doesn't sound like a conspiracy, nothing ever will. But wait! There's more!

The game is tied 1-1 at the end of regulation and goes into overtime. Brazil scores in the third minute on a play that is clearly offside. The officials miss the call and the goal stands. The U.S. can't buy a break!

So there they were. There *we* were. A goal down. A man down. And only 27 minutes left to play. Compounding our problems was the very bad acting of Brazilian players as they faked one injury after another to milk more time off the clock.

I have never been so incensed watching a game of anything. I love our country and I love this team and they were clearly getting hosed. They deserved better! I was furious over the litany of big decisions that were going against us. I wasn't watching a soccer game on my television; I was watching a heist!

But here's the thing, and it's the only thing that really matters: Those American players who had every right to complain, didn't. They chose a completely different response. They chose a better response. And because of it, I will never let myself succumb to the notion that a referee cost my team a game. If it wasn't for all the adversity that was heaped upon them, there would never have been a moment like Abby Wambach's sensational goal to send the game to penalty kicks. It was one of the greatest, most exciting moments in all of sports. If you haven't seen it, you need to. If you did see it, watch it again; you won't regret it. Go to Youtube and search for Abby Wambach Goal vs. Brazil. Seriously, do it now.

Isn't that the sweetest thing you've ever seen! And wasn't it made so much sweeter precisely *because* of the adversity our team was faced with? I recommend you watch it a second time and listen carefully to the words of the play-by-play commentator as he prematurely predicts the demise of Team USA.

The next time you are tempted to blame the officials for your team's result, remember Megan Rapinoe and Abby Wambach and that U.S. team and their response to a mountain of adversity. That team held itself to a higher standard. You should too. We all should. That team erased every excuse we will ever have.

Don't blame the results (or anything really) on the officials. When you do that you absolve your child of his responsibility to give his very best regardless of the circumstance and of his responsibility to accept the result.

SECTION 4
WHAT YOUR
KID WANTS YOU
TO KNOW

44

Why We Play

Author's Note: Occasionally the office computer flummoxes me to the point that I need to place a call to the I.T. Department. Without fail, at some point in that conversation, the I.T. representative will ask me something about my computer, like how many bits of RAM I am running or whether or not I've checked the flux capacitor. At that point I usually say, "Look, there's a reason I'm a soccer coach. Everything you just said is way above my pay grade."

So before we go any further, let me be perfectly clear that I am not a child psychologist or a behavioral psychologist and my college degree was not in any type of field that relates to childhood development. With the exception of the cited sources, everything you are about to read is anecdotal and purely a matter of my own opinions which have been shaped over the past two decades of coaching and observing kids of all ages. I believe in the opinions I'm about to express, but I don't have the science to back me up. Whether or not you agree with what I've written, well, that's for you to decide.

Now, moving right along…

Soccer combines a list of factors that we are passionate about: sports, winning/losing, and our children. It's a volatile mix. When you combine sports with kids, you've got gunpowder and a fuse. Parents are the matches that can set off an explosion.

Statistics tell us that the chances of your child staying involved in soccer beyond the age of 13 are relatively slim. I want you to make a promise to yourself that if your child quits soccer, it won't be because of you.

To be a Gold Star Soccer Parent, you need to know why your child is playing in the first place. You need to know what motivates him to return to the field week after week. Here is a list of the top reasons that kids play soccer:[1]

- *To have fun*
- *To do something I'm good at*
- *To play as part of a team*
- *To exercise and stay in shape*
- *To learn a new skill*

Those are some excellent reasons for you to support your child's involvement in soccer. What's equally important is what didn't make the list: Winning. Your kid isn't playing soccer to win. I'm sure he enjoys winning much more than losing, but the results aren't why he will or won't stop playing. If winning doesn't make your child's list, then it shouldn't make yours either.

You want your child to stay involved in soccer, right? If you don't, you should. For starters it provides a great deal of exercise and everything in our lives begins with our good health. But there are plenty of other amazing peripheral benefits to playing soccer such as:

- *Learning cooperation and teamwork*
- *Learning accountability and responsibility*
- *Learning how to handle adversity*
- *Learning self-discipline*
- *Learning leadership skills*

- *Learning sportsmanship*
- *Building self-confidence and self-esteem*

If your daughter plays soccer, there are even more reasons to hope that her interest does not fade. We know that females who play sports enjoy higher levels of self-esteem. They have lower levels of depression and obesity. They have a more positive body image than girls who don't play sports. They are three times more likely to graduate high school and they are more likely to have better grades. They are more likely to go to college. They are 92% less likely to use drugs and they are less likely to stay in an abusive relationship. They are 80% less likely to have an unintended pregnancy.[2] Do you really need any more reasons to pray like crazy that your daughter doesn't quit!

Okay, now we know why we should want our sons and daughters to stay in soccer for as long as possible. So how exactly are we screwing it up?

Well, the short answer is that we've become over-involved. Our maternal/paternal instincts tell us to fight for our kids and to instruct them on how to do everything better. It's not enough for our children to merely participate; we also want them to achieve!

Here is a list of the top reasons why kids quit playing soccer[3]:

- *Stopped being fun*
- *Lack of playing time*
- *Too much emphasis on winning*
- *Adult behaviors (coaches and parents)*
- *Dissatisfaction with performance*
- *Lack of social support*
- *Other interests*

We could actually make 'Stopped Being Fun' the heading for that list and then slide everything else underneath it. Sure, maybe your kid discovers he has a natural passion for playing the guitar and decides his time is better spent preparing to be a rock star. If that's the case, then that's just fine. But if he discovers another interest, it may also be because the joy was being sucked out of soccer.

You'll notice that lack of playing time is a big factor, and I'm sure that you're sniffing out a contradiction from the What Your Coach Wants You to Know section. You may be saying, *"Well if my kid isn't getting enough playing time and that's going to make her quit, I need to speak up to the coach on her behalf."* No, that's not what I'm saying. Not at all.

Your daughter does not control her playing time and neither do you. Only her coach controls that. What you need to understand is that for your daughter, playing is more important than winning (you'll notice that *losing* wasn't on the list of why kids quit). So instead of focusing your energy on what your daughter won't get on her current team, maybe you should consider finding her a place to play that is better suited to her abilities. She'll be happier playing soccer on a lesser team than she will be sitting the bench on a great team. You have to remember that, more than anything else, soccer players want to actually *play* soccer.

To be a Gold Star Soccer Parent, all you really need to remember is the top line of the list of reasons why kids quit: *It stopped being fun.* Then you just have to figure out the behaviors that suck the fun out of the game for them and then avoid those behaviors at all costs. So, how can you prevent yourself from becoming a fun-sucker? Read on!

45

Remember Whose Game It Is

First of all, remember that soccer is their thing, not yours. The more you involve yourself in it, the greater your chance of sucking the fun from it.

When I was a kid growing up in Trenton, NJ, my buddies and I had a habit of building forts. We'd find whatever lumber we could rustle up and then get into dad's hammer and nails and start building. We had no plan or blueprint. We would just start building. And through the summers of 1976-80, we built one awful fort after another. I mean these things were hideous, but they gave us our own space, a space where we could congregate without adults, and we loved them.

One Saturday morning we started building one of these forts in my friend Bill's backyard. Bill's dad wandered out before we got too far along and he foresaw the calamity that was about to be erected in his backyard. Realizing that we could build a much better fort with his help (and salvage the appearance of his backyard), he installed himself as foreman and took over the project. Bill's dad raised our fort-building to a whole new level. He actually used tools! And not just the hammer! He had saws and saw horses and screw drivers and wrenches! He was out there sawing lumber and using a drill and doing all types of things we had never even considered. It was amazing to sit there and watch him work. Which is exactly what we did – watch.

By the end of the day we had ourselves the best fort any group of neighborhood boys could ever want. For the first time ever our fort had a door that actually opened and closed on hinges! This fort looked nothing like anything we had ever built. The walls stood up straight and there were no random nails jutting out through the wood. This was the way a fort was supposed to look! Our fort totally rocked!

And you know what? About an hour later, we abandoned it. That fort wasn't ours; it belonged to Bill's dad. He was the one who built the whole thing. For us kids, the joy was in the process, not the result. And although the end result was clearly superior, the process was no fun at all. Fort-building was *our thing* and despite his really wonderful intentions, Bill's dad had sucked the fun out of it for us.

Bill's dad made a mistake that most parents make at some point or another; he wanted to contribute to a kids' thing and ended up taking it over. Haven't we all done that somewhere along the line?

The immense growth in skateboarding's popularity is attributed partly to the fact that it was a parent-free sport. Parents couldn't contribute (or judge or critique) because none of them had ever stepped on a skateboard. It was a revolution that was being engineered by daring teenagers who couldn't seem to conform and who wanted to pursue a passion without the interference of adults. Jumping on a skateboard was their way of expressing themselves through an avenue that was totally alien to their parents. It didn't matter how good or bad you were because playing time wasn't a factor. As long as you had a board, you could ride. It was a beautiful, adult-free existence! Doesn't it make perfect sense that so many kids gravitated to the skateboarding culture?

There's an interesting documentary called *DogTown n Z Boyz* that helps trace the cultural phenomena of skateboarding. In the movie, Fran Richards of Transworld Skate Magazine explains the skateboarding boom by saying, "*It isn't a ball and stick sport. It isn't about winning or losing; it's about the process. It's not about the ends; it's about the means.*" We'd all do well to remember that and apply it to our own children as they make their journey through the world of youth sports.

Kids want to solve their own problems; it's one of the joys of growing up. Most parents know this and try to create environments where their children can and will solve their own problems. But for whatever reason, when we get to the field on Saturday morning and see those shiny uniforms and see those corner flags waving in the breeze, we are overcome by the pageantry and we suddenly feel obligated to help those kids solve their problems. So we all start shouting instructions and pretty soon there's an eight-year-old kid whose head is spinning because 30 different people are telling him what to do and all he really wants to do is hang out with his friends and build a fort of their own.

I started golfing around the time I was 30. I never took a lesson; never read a book on how to be a better golfer. I just kept going out to the range and playing 18 holes whenever I could and eventually my golf game graduated from embarrassing to mediocre to acceptably average.

These days I'm a very average golfer and I take a lot of pride in that because I got to my current level of *expertise* all by myself. And if we're out golfing together, it will probably be pretty easy for you to point out a flaw in my swing that, should I correct it, would knock a few strokes off my round. When you get the urge to make the correction that will help me for years to come, do me a favor and don't. Don't say a word. Just let me continue moving right along in my current state of imperfection. Golf is my problem and I want to keep it that way. I don't want you to flatten out the learning curve for me. I want to keep figuring out this game for myself. And that's how your kid feels about soccer.

Kids definitely want you to come to their games and watch them play. But they don't want you to feed them the answers. They go to practice and spend time working hard to improve and on game day, *they want to show you* what they can do. They want you to be proud of how they are improving. They aren't looking for you to solve the puzzle for them.

Your child may come home from school and ask you for help with his spelling homework. So naturally you help him because you want him to do well. But when it's time for the spelling test, you won't take it for him. You help him prepare for the test, but ultimately, you have to release him to take the test for himself. Soccer is no different. If you want to help with the homework, then go kick a ball around in the backyard with your kid. But that Saturday morning game is his test, not yours.

I once served as Technical Director for a club in Montgomery County, Maryland. The club produced a pamphlet for parents to help guide their behaviors. Malcolm Lawrence, the pamphlet's author, drew a wonderful comparison between soccer and school because both of those entities put children in a position to solve problems. When it comes to coaching from the sideline, Malcolm told the parents: When the teacher asks your kid what's two plus two, you wouldn't stand in the hallway yelling, "*Four! The answer is four!*" It makes perfect sense, doesn't it? If you want your kids to grow and learn, you have to give them the chance to solve their own problems. That won't happen if you're constantly trying to feed them the answers. That principle shouldn't disappear just because someone starts keeping score on Saturday mornings.

What would you think of a woman who stood in the school hallway shouting answers to her son? You'd say she was completely nuts, right? Well guess what; if you're a sideline coach, you are that woman! That's right! You and her are 100% the same! And just because a half-dozen other parents are being sideline coaches, that doesn't absolve you of your responsibility not to follow their lead.

I once coached a college team with several international players on the roster. The father of one of the international girls spent three weeks in the U.S. visiting his very talented daughter and attending all of our games. It quickly became clear that this father fancied himself as a sideline coach.

During the first game, his daughter was playing as a left midfielder, which positioned her along the sideline directly in front of her father. She could hear every word he said and he said an awful lot of them. It was driving the poor girl insane. At halftime she came back to the bench in tears, and this was a game where she had scored and we were already winning 3-0! The remarkable thing was that her father was not rude or nasty; he was just constantly telling her what to do and then critiquing her after every play.

She didn't want her father's coaching. She just wanted to play college soccer in the U.S. and her father was sucking the fun right out of it. Right then we decided that as long as her father was at our games, she would play on the side of the field farthest from him. So she might start a game as right midfielder, and then switch to left midfielder for the second half. Isn't that horribly sad? The father had travelled across a rather large ocean to watch his little girl play soccer and we had to keep the two of them separated by the width of a soccer field... and it was *his daughter's idea!*

Your kid already has a coach. She doesn't want another one. Just like you wouldn't want her to spend two hours shouting at you to raise all-in during your weekly poker game.

Let me give you one other really good reason not to be a sideline coach. Chances are that your kid knows more about soccer than you do. Yep, if you've never played soccer, it won't take long before your child surpasses you in both knowledge and expertise. At that moment, your child has become Paul McCartney. Guess who you are. Let me give you a hint: It rhymes with Loko Tono.

Let me tell you something, soccer is a difficult sport to play. Want to know why you think it's boring on television? It's because those guys make it look so darn easy! You may be athletic, but if you've only played hand-based sports, you know nothing about the level of difficulty involved in mastering a soccer ball. If you'd like to try your luck, I'll give you two very basic technical challenges that you can do on your own while no one is watching.

Challenge 1: Juggle a soccer ball to twenty without letting it touch the ground. And oh, by the way, you can't start with the ball in your hands. You've got to lift it off the ground with your feet. Tell me how many weeks it takes you to get it done. That's right - weeks.

Challenge 2: Set out two markers, eight yards apart. With a soccer ball at your feet, see how many times you can dribble a figure 8 around those markers in 30 seconds. When you are done and realizing that maybe you underestimated the difficulty level of maneuvering a soccer ball, remember that you were doing this under no pressure from an opponent, that the ball never left the ground, and that no one was screaming at you from the sideline. And by the way… how's your heart rate? Now compare your results to that of your child's. Yes, soccer is a lot harder than it looks.

By the age of nine I knew more about soccer than either of my parents. I could play it better than either of them and I knew the rules and strategies better than they did. And I wasn't exactly a soccer savant. Do you have any idea how frustrating it is for a 12-year-old boy who has been playing soccer for 5 years to hear his mom, who has never kicked a ball, telling him what to do on the soccer field? That boy doesn't come to your workplace and tell you how to do your job. Just let him run around and be a kid and figure things out for himself. If he doesn't get all the answers right, the world won't come apart at the seams. So chill the heck out!

If you've been paying attention to your reading, you must have reached the conclusion that there are two distinct entities that don't want you to be a sideline coach: Your coach and your kid. Do everyone a favor and listen to them.

46

My Goals May Be Different Than Yours

I'm going to make this short and sweet. If you signed your kid up for soccer so she can earn a college scholarship, you need to throttle back. Go back a few pages and see why kids play soccer. That's not a list of things I made up. That's a list of answers from actual soccer-playing kids who were asked why they play. Please note that the phrase *college scholarship* does not appear.

It's worth mentioning that, according to the NCAA, only 1 in 56 high school athletes (across all sports) receive some type of college athletic scholarship. Roughly 1 in 90 high school soccer players receive a full scholarship. Only 2% of youth soccer players end up playing college soccer. Your daughter's odds are not exactly stellar, so try to maintain some perspective.

It's great if your child loves soccer enough to have specific soccer goals, but remember that those are her goals, not yours. Your primary goals should be to support her and to keep soccer enjoyable so that she wants to keep playing.

Regardless of how much money you invest into your daughter's travel soccer team, it does not mean she automatically gets a college scholarship. Consider that before you start spending all your money.

47

It's Okay To Fail

One of the problems with giving our children the freedom to fail is that they won't disappoint us. You have to make peace with that. There's an old saying that reads: *That which doesn't kill us only makes us stronger.* Amen.

We become stronger through our failures. We learn from them. And is there any greater satisfaction than when we finally figure out how to overcome them?

When your kid plays soccer, he's going to make mistakes. Awesome! Let him make soccer mistake after soccer mistake because eventually, one day, the light bulb will go on and he will have mastered a new skill. Then he can go on to making and correcting the next mistake.

Can I tell you about my favorite round of golf? It was the first time I ever golfed 18 holes without losing a ball. Sounds silly, right? Well, not to me. When I first started golfing I sprayed golf balls around the course like an atomic Pez dispenser. It wasn't uncommon for me to lose a dozen or more balls in a day. I once lost seven balls on the first stinkin' hole! Seriously! So I set a goal that one day I would complete a round of golf with one, single ball.

I can't begin to imagine how many times I failed, and failed miserably, to reach that goal. I habitually had to borrow a golf ball or two just to finish a round. If we played a hole that was adjacent to the driving range, I would scoop up as many range balls as I could and stick them in my bag. On many days I was the guy hitting the ball that had the red stripe. But on one glorious afternoon in Daytona Beach, FL, all the stars aligned for me and I played an entire 18 holes with a single ball – and I could not have been happier! I wasn't just happy; I was proud! Darn proud! I had reached my goal and I had done it all by myself! It doesn't matter how old or young you are, reaching the goals you set for yourself feels absolutely fantastic!

Failure is not fatal, and that also applies to your kids. You don't always have to rescue them and quite frankly, when it comes to soccer, they'd prefer it if you didn't. Soccer is a wonderfully imperfect game and your child is going to make mistakes – lots of them. Fantastic! With each mistake he is one step closer to the solution. Encourage him to keep making mistakes because eventually he's going to figure it out. And when he does, he'll be a better soccer player and a more confident, self-reliant person.

Soccer is a wonderful microcosm of life. On and off the field, we will all fail many, many times before it's all said and done, but we are not measured by our failures; we are measured by our ability to respond to those failures. We are measured by our perseverance, our ability to get knocked down and then stand back up and keep moving forward. The ability to respond to our failures isn't just a soccer skill; it's a life skill, and one of the most important of all. The person who quits at the first sign of failure is ill-equipped to function as an adult in the real world.

One of the great things about sports is that they give the players a stage to showcase their resilience. When you keep jumping in to save the day, you rob them of that stage. You rob them of that opportunity to showcase their toughness and determination and their ability to face adversity and solve their own problems. That's not your job. If your kid needs to be rescued, he'll let you know. In the meantime, sit back, take a deep breath and let him fail, fail, fail! It's the way of the Gold Star Soccer Parent.

48

Reflections

We know that winning isn't the reason that kids play sports, and we know that losing isn't the reason that most of them quit. Then why can't we, as parents, do a better job of separating our own emotions from the performance of our children?

Before we go any further, let me be perfectly clear that I'm not the tree-hugging, hippie-type who thinks that winning doesn't matter. I do believe kids should be taught to compete their hardest and that they should do everything in their power to try and win, and that includes pushing right up against the edge of the rules. As far as I'm concerned, if it's worth playing, it's worth winning. I think in many ways, in our desire to protect our children from any hardship whatsoever, we've overreacted and over-corrected and we are producing a softer brand of athlete and person and a nation of teenagers that feel entitled to have any obstruction to their instant gratification immediately vaporized from whatever space it is occupying.

I don't agree with leagues that don't keep score. I've never understood that concept. If a group of seven-year-olds get together to play a game of anything, you can bet they are going to keep score. Keeping score is fun because it gives the participants something to aim for. Why would anyone take winning out of soccer? The goal in soccer is literally the goal of soccer.

You don't build a child's self-esteem by sheltering her from every emotional setback, and in soccer, there are definitely going to be some setbacks. You can't hand out self-esteem. It's not candy. Study after study has taught us that. Self-esteem is earned. It is the result of achieving actual accomplishments, not artificial ones; and kids are actually smart enough to know the difference.

Winning is great and it's way better than losing and more often than not the players who try the hardest to win actually do win. I don't see any problem with that philosophy as it tends to reappear frequently throughout the entirety of this little thing we call life. As parents, what we absolutely must remember is that the results, good or bad, don't belong to us. The results belong to the kids who play the game. (Read those last two sentences again. Go ahead. I'll wait.)

One of the reasons that parents get so fixated on the result of a kids' game is that we see our children as a reflection of ourselves; and don't we all hold ourselves in pretty high regard? When I watch my daughter play, I honestly don't care if she can't kick or trap a ball. But what makes me cringe is when Izzy ducks away from a ball, or when she doesn't go in hard to take the ball from an opponent. It pains me to see this type of passive behavior because it's the opposite of who I am. As a soccer player, I see myself as fearless and aggressive and ultra-competitive, and I genuinely like that those are my signature qualities.

But Izzy just isn't wired that way. She's a different person. Heck, when you get right down to it, she's a better person. She just wants to put on her uniform and run around with her friends and hug people. The moment the game ends, all she is thinking about is the post-game snack and getting home to see her puppies. I've come to realize that her outlook on life is probably a lot more conducive to happiness than mine. Still, I can't help but bow my head and rub my temples when she ducks out of the way of a bouncing ball.

I've had to make peace with the fact that Izzy is not me and that her performance is not a reflection of me. She's her and I'm me and that's just how it goes. As much as I'd like her to be the holy terror of Oconee County U10 rec soccer, it ain't happening. Not today. Not tomorrow. Not ever. But it doesn't affect how I feel about her. Nor should it.

Even though it's been my career, on Saturday mornings, soccer is Izzy's thing and I've got to maintain a separation between her soccer world and mine. And believe me, it's not always easy. Sometimes I just have to remind myself of all those reasons I want to have a soccer-playing daughter. Then the picture becomes a lot clearer.

Izzy is not a mini-me. And your kid is not a mini-you. They are not adults running around disguised as children. They are kids playing a kids' game. When you fixate on their performance, you take that away from them.

Many parents, particularly those with no soccer background, see their reflections more on the scoreboard than in their own child's performance. If you are one of these parents, you are skating on some wafer-thin ice.

When you get married to the scoreboard, you and your child are in for some rocky times. Soccer can be a cruel, cruel game, and more than any other sport, in soccer, the better team loses. If you are genuinely invested in whether or not your seven-year-old wins her game this weekend, you need to take a big step back. Then another one. And another.

Can I ask you this: Who freaking cares? Who cares if your kid's team gets clobbered 7-0? What does it matter in the grand scheme? Yes, I know you don't want your kid to lose, but is it really that great of a calamity? When that game ends, how does your life change? Will you suddenly lose your job or develop acne? Will your stock portfolio plummet? Of course not. Why? Because it's just some kids playing soccer and nobody should care who wins and who loses except the kids who are playing the game.

Incidentally, if you think that this is only an issue if your team loses, wow are you missing the boat! Let's turn this situation inside out.

In your first game of the season, your daughter scored a goal in the final minute to win the game. Awesome, right? You're proud and excited and you can't wait to update your Facebook status to tell the world how much your kid completely rocks! As soon as the game is over you pick her up and swing her around and tell her how amazing she is and that you're going straight out to celebrate with some Fro-Yo. Everything is coming up roses!

So here's my question: How are you going to react a week later when your kid inadvertently knocks the ball into her own goal to lose the game? Are you going to be less excited to see her? Are you going to tell the world how she lost the game with an own-goal and how great she is anyway? Are you still going for Fro-Yo?

Yeah, it's pretty impossible to hide your emotions under those types of extremes, but you have to be careful. Do you love your kid more when she wins and less when she loses? Do you love her more when she scores and less when she doesn't? Of course you don't! Make sure that your child is getting that message loud and clear. You don't want your daughter associating the result of a soccer game with how much her parents love her. It puts an immense amount of emotional pressure on a child when she feels that mommy and daddy will love her less if she doesn't win or doesn't score. That's the type of pressure a parent can put on a child without even realizing it. That's how even the most well-intentioned soccer parents can end up as fun-suckers.

Fun-suckers are not just those world class idiots we hear about from time to time who go completely mental on the sideline and start a battle royal. Those lunatics make up a tiny fraction of soccer parents, and we know a much greater percentage of soccer parents have kids who will quit by the age of 13. The kids who quit aren't just the ones with over-the-top, loudmouthed, knuckleheads for parents. Most fun-suckers have no idea whatsoever of how they are bleeding the fun from their child's experience. Soccer parents have to find a level of consistency in how they treat their child when the game ends, regardless of the child's performance and regardless of the result.

When I was a much younger coach, I would get really emotionally invested in my team's performance. It wasn't so much about whether we were winning or losing, but if my team was playing poorly, I would feel a sense of embarrassment because in my eyes, they looked poorly coached and that was a reflection of me. That feeling of failure would eat away at my insides like a plate of bad clams. Then one day I figured it out.

Soccer isn't a joystick sport like baseball, football or basketball, where the coach can have a huge impact on every single pitch, play or possession. Soccer is a player's game and once it starts, there's not a whole heckuva lot that the coach can do except sit back and watch. In soccer, the real coaching is done in the days and weeks leading up to the game. When I finally made peace with that, I came to the realization that on game day there were many, many factors beyond my control and I could not hold myself responsible for all of them. So I made myself a deal: I would do the very best job I possibly could to prepare my team, and then I would release myself of responsibility from the things that were beyond my control on game day. To make a long story short, I decided that the best I could hope for was a clear conscience when the game kicked off. If I had a clear conscience about the preparation I had given my team, well, I couldn't control if they went out there and stunk up the field. Once I began focusing more on the preparation and less on the performance, I became a much calmer coach and person.

Do yourself a favor and do your child a bigger one: Accept the fact that the result just isn't that important to your kid. So if it's your kid's thing and not yours, and the result doesn't matter that much to your child, it really shouldn't matter to you at all. All you really need is a clear conscience before the game even begins. Your child is not a mini-you. Separate yourself from your child's performance and the result, and give a consistent message.

49

Beware The Car Ride Home

When Izzy first said she wanted to play soccer, I made her agree to three rules:

1. *Give your very best effort*
2. *Have fun*
3. *Don't complain*

She has to tell me those three things before each game and practice session. But that's the easy part. Before she gets to the field we are both excited and happy and filled with optimism. What actually happens once the game begins, well, that can be a whole different can of peaches — especially if things didn't go as we had hoped. As parents, the time between the final whistle and unlocking our front door can be a tremendous test of our better angels. We must be very sensitive to the importance of that delicate time slot.

Young players are extremely resilient and they don't dwell on results. Ten seconds after the final whistle blows, win or lose, a nine-year-old is ready to move on to other things. Please let him.

The car ride home is a hard-hat area, particularly if the parent can't let go of the game, the officiating, the result, or the player's performance. Players who stop having fun, quit. And when you ask them to pinpoint why they stopped having fun, the car ride home is commonly at the top of their list. Would you believe that the car ride home can be a traumatic experience for your child?

When a game ends, your kid quickly changes out of his super-hero, soccer player identity and back into his regular identity as a normal kid. You've got to make that same transition. I know this can be really difficult, especially if you're competitive by nature, but you have to remember that soccer is not your thing; it belongs to your child and it belongs to him alone.

My daughter's soccer games are a 20-minute ride from our house. That's an awfully long ride when I don't feel Izzy worked very hard during the second half. I've got 20 minutes to stew in my frustration that my little girl didn't give her best effort. It's especially frustrating because I know that unlike most soccer parents, I'm genuinely qualified to help her. So I have to sit there biting my tongue until my eyes are ready to pop out of my head. Why? Because that's what she needs me to do. That's what is in her best interest and it's the best way to keep me from being a fun-sucker. I may have blood coming out of my ears, but I refuse to talk about the game unless Izzy brings it up first. And you know what? She NEVER does!

Sure it's incredibly frustrating, but I've got to be a big boy and not cave to my own ego. Soccer is her thing. It's her fort and she gets to decide whether or not to invite me inside. Strangely enough, it was Izzy who taught me the best lesson about how to act after a game when she was just six.

In August of 2010, I experienced my first game as a soccer coach at the University of Georgia. We had our home opener against Duke in front of 2,300 people. It was an incredible atmosphere and as that game kicked off and I looked across the field at all those spectators, all I could think was, *Holy cow, I've finally made it!*

My expectations for that game were immense. Duke was one of the premier teams in the nation. If we won that game, it would give me a tremendous sense of satisfaction and joy and confidence that after all these years, yes, I really did know what the heck I was doing.

It was a fantastic game! Duke was the better team in the first half and scored a goal. We were the better team in the second half and did not. Duke won 1-0. It was fair result after an exceptionally hard-fought match between two very good teams. And yet I was devastated. Not only had we lost, we had also failed to score. 2,300 people came to see us win and we didn't even score a stinkin' goal. It was beyond demoralizing. It was heartbreaking.

That was the first college soccer game that Izzy ever saw. My wife had dressed her in a Georgia cheerleading outfit and painted a 'G' on her cheek. Izzy was so excited to be a Georgia Bulldog and even more excited to cheer on her daddy's team. I can't tell you how much I wanted that little girl to see us win.

After the game I had to walk back across the field to get into the building that houses our soccer offices. Izzy was waiting for me just outside the door with her arms wide open, waiting for a great big daddy hug. I picked up my little girl, gave her a hug, kissed her on each cheek, then set her down and went inside to finish up my duties for the night.

An hour later we were sitting in the pizza joint that's down the road from our stadium. I wasn't very talkative because I was still in a funk about the game. Izzy walked over, gave me another hug, patted me on the back and said, *"It's okay, Daddy."* That was it. That was all she said. She never asked me about the game. She never asked in the car on the way to get pizza, and she didn't ask when we were at the restaurant. She never asked why we didn't win. She didn't ask me that night or any night since, and we've had four seasons together. It doesn't matter if we win or lose the game, Izzy is just happy to see her Daddy.

Now doesn't that sound like exactly the type of family member you'd want to see after a game? *Believe me*, it is. It most certainly is! It's also exactly the type of family member your child wants greeting him after the game.

I once had the opportunity to hear Bruce Brown speak. Bruce is one of the founders of Proactive Coaching and he has been a tremendous advocate on behalf of the children who play youth sports. He spent 35 years coaching a variety of sports from the junior high to collegiate levels and is one of the most sought after speakers on the topic of youth sports. Bruce was adamant about the importance of parents not resuscitating a game that has already died, and he emphasized that parents must be particularly mindful of the danger zone that is the car ride home.

Bruce's research tells us that if you're going to say something, say this: *I love watching you play.*

'*I love watching you play*' is both positive and consistent. It is a beautiful, judgment free statement that your opinion of your child and the love you feel for him does not fluctuate with the scoreboard. It lets your child know that you support him unconditionally and that even when he didn't have his best day, you've still got his back.

After each of Izzy's games, before we get into the car, I try to mention one moment where she did something particularly well, specifically in terms of her effort or courage. The way I see it, her soccer ability will only take her so far, so I want to reinforce the values that will be applicable in her life beyond the game.

There will be those days when your child may actually want to talk about the game in the car, particularly as he gets older. That's fine; just be careful. This can be a giant trap if you don't handle the situation with diplomacy. Tread carefully and remember the story I'm about to share with you.

Many years ago I met a girl who volunteered as a counselor on a suicide hotline. I told her that I would be awful in her job. I told her that I wouldn't know what to say to someone on the verge of killing himself.

She literally laughed at me and, more specifically, my stupidity. She said that people who are on the verge of suicide don't call to hear what you have to say; they call to find someone who will *listen to them*. I've never forgotten that lesson and it's come in handy many times over the course of my adult life.

If your child wants to talk about the game in the car, it doesn't give you carte blanche to unload all of your infinite wisdom on how he could be better, how the coach could be better, and how the team could be better. If your boy wants to talk soccer, feel free to indulge him and support him. But make sure it is his idea and remember that story about the suicide hotline operator. Soccer is his thing, not yours. If he wants to talk about the game, then it's because *he* wants to talk about the game. He's not necessarily asking for your input or assessment. Do your best to be a listener, not a talker, and help him talk himself out.

If you're talking soccer after the game, try asking questions like:

- *What was your favorite part of the game?*
- *What do you think your team did well?*
- *Is there anything you want to work on to improve?*

These types of questions give your child the chance to reflect on the game and on his individual performance and to discover his own answers. That's a much better alternative than asking why he gave the ball away or why he missed that one great chance to score.

Do not underestimate the power of the car ride home. It's like a room with a gas leak. Make sure you don't light the match that blows up everyone. Use great caution. If you're not careful, your son is going to quit soccer and take up skateboarding.

50

Share The Passion

I hope that I haven't been misunderstood. I don't want you to think that I don't see the value in creating an environment where your soccer player will be driven to excel and outdistance the competition. If that's the message you've gotten, then I haven't done a very good job of communicating my stance. I think it's completely awesome when a person of any age finds something they are passionate about and then commits to achieving at a high level in that endeavor. That's totally admirable. What I'd like you to remember is the connection between passion and commitment. Rarely will you get the latter if the former isn't already in place.

Kids are all wired differently and soccer is going to mean different things to each of them. For some it will never be more than an enjoyable way to spend time with friends. For others it will be as important as eating and more important than school. If your child falls into the latter category, I'm not suggesting you dial her down (although your future may include paying for some tutors).

If your daughter wants to work harder than everyone else, let her! If she wants to compete like a lion and annihilate her opponents, encourage her! If she wants to play until her feet bleed through her shoes, celebrate her! And if she genuinely hates to lose, please don't talk her out of it! Some kids are born to compete and that's a pretty useful quality in athletics. But remember, you can encourage her, steer her, guide her and drive her, but if she's ever going to be great at soccer, she'll first have to love playing it. The best thing you can do is help grow her love for the game; only then will she get interested in mastering it.

Would you like to know an easy way to further your cause as a Gold Star Soccer Parent? Go play soccer in the backyard with your kid. If your backyard isn't an option, then go to a local park. Go to a schoolyard. Go anywhere you can find a decent-sized patch of grass, put a ball on the ground and play with your kid. And saying that you don't know how to kick a ball isn't a good enough excuse.

Your kid doesn't always need you to be the expert. Kids love playing ball with their parents! You don't have to be any good. You just have to be willing to spend some time engaging in an activity where you may not have any technical competence. But don't worry! You'll get better at it. As a matter of fact, your kid will be happy to teach you a thing or two. At some point he's going to ask you to play goalie so he can shoot. Do it!

This is an especially fantastic idea when your child first begins his soccer experience. Joining a new team in a new sport is a lot like the first day of class at a new school; it can be pretty intimidating. The more competent your child is, the better he will feel about his experience. Help your son with some of the basics. In soccer, that means kicking, dribbling and trapping a ball, and those things are just a matter of repetition. The more competent a player is, the more likely he is to enjoy his soccer experience and want to continue along with it.

You can also foster your child's passion and competence by taking him to watch soccer games. Help him become a fan of the game. Kids who love any sport are fascinated when they watch it being played by older players. The game is faster and more physical and that has a lot of Wow factor in the eyes of an eleven-year-old. You don't have to bust the bank and go to see a professional match. Go watch a local high school, college or junior college game. If you go on a regular basis, your son will begin to identify his favorite players and he'll start trying to emulate them. This is a good thing. When your son adds *soccer fan* to his life as a soccer player, his love for the game will continue to grow, as will his competence.

Having sat on the sideline of college soccer games for the past two decades, I've had the opportunity to observe the really cool phenomena of ball-kids. Ball-kids (a.k.a. ball-shaggers) are the kids who stand around the perimeter of the field to retrieve the balls that go out of bounds. Let me assure you that having the opportunity to participate as a ball-shagger is a big, big deal to these kids because it's like having a backstage pass to the biggest show in town. Ball-shaggers get to be closer to the action than anyone in the stadium; they get to hear things that the coaches say on the bench and the players say on the field; they get to be right up close with the players; and they get to actively participate in the periphery of the match. It's an incredible fly-on-the-wall experience, except these flies actually get to interact with the players.

When our ball-kids show up before the game, I can't explain how excited they are to be taking part in a college soccer match. These kids are smiling from ear to ear. They are getting an experience that their friends at school aren't getting, and that makes it very special.

The ball-shagger experience has a bigger effect than you might realize. I know because in the late 70s and early 80s I was the preeminent ball-shagger for the Mercer County Community College men's soccer team. It was epic! Before long the players knew me by name and when a college soccer player is calling a ten-year-old by name, I assure you it's a very big deal to the ten-year-old.

While I was roaming the sidelines, my dad was watching from the bleachers. When the games ended, I couldn't wait to tell him all the cool stuff I heard down at field-level. Then on the ride home we would talk about the game and how much we enjoyed seeing some player do whatever it was he did and how the ref missed that one call and what a great goal so-and-so scored.

That experience as a ball-shagger fueled my drive to keep playing and improving, and I assure you that I am not the only one. I don't have any data to back me up on this, but I am certain that the vast majority of players who have regularly served as ball-girls for my teams have stuck with soccer well beyond the age of 13. These days I occasionally hear from some of them and they all tell me that their experience as ball-shaggers had a lot to do with their love for soccer. Do not underestimate the impact that this experience can have on your young soccer player.

If your kid wants to volunteer as a ball-shagger, just pick up the phone and call the coach. Teams are always on the hunt for ball-shaggers and nothing beats free labor. If you can't get a hold of the coach, then show up 30 minutes before kick-off and ask him. Just make sure your kid understands how to do the job and knows that ball-shaggers actually play an important role, especially when it's late in a close game. Ball-shaggers are expected to run, not walk, after a ball that's gone out of bounds. A ball-shagger who falls asleep at the wheel will likely get an earful from a player who is in a hurry to get the ball back in play.

If you can't make the commitment of going to see games live, I suggest spending some time in front of the television. For decades, coaches in the U.S. have lamented the fact that their players don't watch enough soccer on television. We used to be able to blame that on television because soccer matches were hardly ever broadcast. These days, that's not the case. The English Premier League, the MLS, the NWSL and a wide array of international matches and tournaments are broadcast virtually around the clock. Today's players have the chance to watch the best players in the world and then try to model their skill sets. If your child is watching a soccer game on Saturday morning, don't roll your eyes and groan before deciding it's a good time to mow the lawn. Instead, why not sit down alongside him and take an interest in what he's doing? Watch the game and ask him to explain some of the things you don't understand. If a kid can learn a lot about soccer by watching it on TV, then his parents can too!

If soccer is your kid's passion, you can help nourish that passion by stepping out of your comfort zone and spending time doing something he loves to do. Of course, if you'd rather just buy him a skateboard...

51

She Actually Likes These People

You've read why your coach thinks it's an awful idea to compare your daughter to her teammates. You should know that your child wholeheartedly agrees with him.

Your daughter is forging relationships with her coach and her teammates. She knows them on a level that you never will and she values their friendships. She values their opinions of her. They are important people in her life whether you like it or not. When you speak badly of her coach or her teammates, you are inadvertently putting her in a position to choose between them and you, and that's a choice she doesn't want to make. It's also a choice she shouldn't have to make. Although you are trying to position yourself as your daughter's ally, in actuality you are burying her under a new kind of stress.

When you try to sway your daughter's opinion of her coach or teammates in a negative way, you are asking her to betray them. It puts her in a horribly uncomfortable position that she'd prefer to avoid. When you tell her that Jenny is awful and that she's killing the team's chances of winning, your own daughter is squirming in her seat. You may be right; Jenny may be awful and your daughter might very well know it. It still doesn't matter. Jenny is a good kid and your daughter likes her regardless of whether or not she can trap a soccer ball. For your daughter, friendship trumps results, which really isn't the worst outlook a kid can have on life. And although she may not say it out loud, your daughter knows what you're doing is wrong and she doesn't like it one bit. You're painting her into a corner where sticking up for her friend means being disloyal to you. Do you really think a 12-year-old should have to make that choice? Of course you don't. Do you know the easiest way for her to avoid making that choice between family and friend? That's right – she can quit.

Remember, soccer is her thing, not yours. Don't inject your negative opinions of others, even if you think that you're doing it to further your daughter's cause. Your intentions may be good, but they are certainly not wise. Sometimes it's just best to remember the old adage: *if you can't say something nice, then don't say anything at all.*

52

Be Seen And Not Heard (Much)

Someone very wise once said that sports do not build character, they reveal it. Believe me; as a sideline parent, your character will be revealed.

Yes, your kid wants you to be at the games and she wants you to cheer for her *and* her teammates. And come to think of it, that's about all she wants. What she absolutely doesn't want; what will scar her for years and ensure her future as a seventy-five-percenter, is when you become the center of attention, even for just a moment.

If you want to know why the retention rate in youth sports is so low, you really need to look no farther than the sidelines. Parents have a way of turning a kids' soccer game into a battle of the gladiators in the Coliseum. The importance we assign to these games is unfathomable! And for all the years I've spent doing this, all I can really say is that I just don't get it.

When my buddies and I played football or Wiffle Ball in the backyard, no parents showed up to cheer us on or scream about the officiating or to take over the construction of our fort. It was fantastic! We picked our own teams and established the boundaries and the rules. Everyone got to play, we competed hard, we got dirty and sweaty and often times bloody. We often argued and sometimes we fought. There were winners and losers and we played until someone got called home for dinner. To us, the games were competitive and exciting and the world hung on every play. But there was never a parent to be found. They were content to let us be.

Why do parents suddenly lose the plot the moment the sport becomes 'organized?' Where was all that *passion* during our three hour games of Nerf football? Is it any surprise that we played hundreds of those games when we were growing up? Are parents really so overwhelmed by the formality and pageantry of a youth soccer game that we completely lose sight of our priorities and forget what is right and wrong? Is it because we had to get into the car and drive to the game that we somehow feel entitled to be satisfied with the outcome? Do we feel that our stature in the community is influenced by a game between our children? If we can go without interfering in a game of Wiffle Ball, why can't we do the same for a game of soccer?

Your sideline behavior is going to be a major factor in whether or not your child continues to play soccer. Your voice doesn't just blend into the chorus of other parents. It cuts through those voices and seeks out your daughter's ear. If she can hear it, she's going to assume her teammates and coaches and refs and opponents can hear it also. And heaven forbid you shout at one of her teammates, because for any child, that is genuinely mortifying! Although the game might be taking place on a Saturday, your daughter is going to see a lot of those other kids in school on Monday morning, a lot of them are going to be her friends, and she's going to experience some social backlash. She doesn't want you shouting at her teammates or coaches or the referees or even the opponents.

When you go to your kid's game, I don't care how far you drove or how much you paid in league dues, you aren't entitled to a thing. You're not at Yankee Stadium. You're not at a sports bar on an NFL Sunday screaming at a television. You are a guest at that game and your behavior should reflect that. If you want to cheer for your child and her team, great! Just make sure you are cheering for her team and not against the opponent. And as much as you may want to vent, don't. Just don't. Learn to swallow those words. A day later you'll be glad you did. Years later your child will thank you for not being like So and So's loud-mouth father.

Let me give you another of Bruce Brown's pearls of wisdom:

You can play. You can coach. You can officiate. You can be a fan. But you need to pick just one and respect the others. Know your role.

If you want to be a Gold Star Soccer Parent on the sideline, heed this advice for the third time: Less is more. If you're on the sideline and you're not sure whether or not you should say what you're about to say, remember these words our teachers used to tell us: *If you wouldn't want it to appear on the front page of tomorrow's newspaper, don't do it.*

There's a lot of wisdom in those words but to be fair, when I was a kid, you had to do something pretty remarkable to end up in the newspaper. In today's culture there's a whole new newspaper that you can end up in rather easily, and it's called YouTube. And once you're on it, you're on it forever.

I think the best way for coaches, teams and leagues to shape sideline behavior is to film it. Set up a camera to film the parents and make sure they know it's there. People tend to be on their best behavior when they know they're on camera.

So before you berate a ref or shout at a player, ask if you'd want to see yourself acting like that on YouTube. Because you just might. If you need some proof, just go to YouTube and search for Soccer Parent. Then ask yourself if that is how you want your child — *and the world* - to see you.

53

Curb Your Enthusiasm

Yes, even if you are saying all the right things and none of the wrong ones, you still need to be mindful of your surroundings. An over-enthusiastic parent can ruin the game for everyone. No kid wants to be known as the one with the crazy mom who runs up and down the sidelines cheering like a lunatic, screaming her son's name every ten seconds. By that same token, your fellow spectators won't appreciate the crazy mom act either. Learn to contain yourself. You don't have to behave like you're at the library, but at least show some restraint. The other parents came to see the show; not to spend the game distracted by the mom who can't sit still.

This is equally important when your child's team is winning, and specifically if his team is winning by a wide margin. At a certain point, you should start dialing down your celebrations after a goal is scored. Remember that the thing you are celebrating is actually painful for about half the people on your sideline. There's a fine line between celebrating and rubbing it in, and the fans who are losing ultimately decide where that line is. Make sure that your celebrations aren't antagonizing the less fortunate half of the spectators.

Let me provide you with a little perspective. I started playing soccer in 1975 and coaching it in 1991, so I've personally been a part of nearly 2,000 games. We can also factor in the thousand or so games I've watched at tournaments or on the recruiting trail, and several hundred games I've seen on television. That's a lot of games, right? Well, in all of those games I've never seen a team that led by five goals not win the game. As a matter of fact, only twice have I seen a team come back from four goals down to tie a game. In soccer, short of a miracle, when a team establishes a four-goal lead, the game is over for all intents and purposes. A five-goal lead is officially a rout.

Yes, I know that you're genuinely excited that your team scored another goal, but apply some tact to your reactions. No one likes having someone dance upon his kid's grave, including that guy sitting next to you. Don't poke at a raw nerve. Recognize when it's time to dial down your exuberance.

54

The Meltdown

There you are, a mile from your exit, desperately wanting to get off that highway, but you know that won't be happening anytime soon. You're in a quagmire of two lanes of standstill traffic and in the past ten minutes you've moved about ten feet. You are losing your patience. The little devil appears on your shoulder and starts saying, *"Hey pal, why not jump on over into the shoulder lane? You can be home in five minutes."* But on your other shoulder, your better angel is shouting him down, reminding you that the right thing to do and the easy thing to do are often not one in the same. You're a good person and a good citizen and you're going to stay put and obey the law and wait this one out.

After a few more minutes of going nowhere, a car that was just a half-mile behind you cruises by in the shoulder, headed exactly where you want to go and certain to get there well ahead of you. You shake your head and mutter, *"Jerk."* Fifteen seconds later a second car whizzes by you; and then a third and a fourth. Eventually you've had enough of being the good guy. Why should you be punished for doing the right thing while these other knuckleheads are rewarded for doing the wrong thing?

When the environment surrounding a soccer game turns ugly, it usually follows that same pattern. A bunch of *good* parents get tired of listening to a single bozo, and then it all deteriorates from there. Just like in the traffic jam, a single instigator leads everyone down the wrong lane. Then we have a total meltdown. It may be disappointing, but it's really not all that surprising. It's just an unfortunate part of human nature.

People are contagious. We all have energy and our energy will spill over to the people next to us. When that energy is magnified by the emotion of competition, it can turn into a pretty nasty brew. It was true when you heard it in first grade and it's still true now: *One bad apple can spoil the bunch.*

If at all possible, put the bad apples out of earshot. Yeah, it's a little inconvenient to pick up your chair and move to the other end of the field, but sometimes ignorance really is bliss. You'll have a much more enjoyable experience when you can't hear the instigators. Sometimes repositioning yourself will solve the problem. Unfortunately, sometimes it won't.

I'm happy to say that there has never been a true knucklehead at one of Izzy's games and I sincerely hope that there never will be. As much as I'd like to tell you that I would be able to restrain myself if some idiot yelled something nasty at my daughter, I doubt I'm that noble. The challenge we all face is to prevent the problem before it starts, because once there's an actual problem, it's really difficult getting the toothpaste back in the tube.

So how do we prevent the problems? Well, we think globally and act locally. Let's start with ourselves. Let's start by figuring out how we are going to treat our own children before, during and after a game. Then let's decide how we're going to treat her teammates, coaches, opponents, parents and referees. Let's make a plan and commit to it. Good soccer parents are just as contagious as the bad ones. Let's remember that the game belongs to the kids, and let's remember all the reasons we want them to keep playing. And let's commit to not being the reason that any of them quit.

You should re-read that last paragraph. It summarizes everything we've been talking about and it's only nine short sentences. If we can all commit to those nine sentences, we're practically home.

Still, the day may come when you run into the idiot who never saw that paragraph. What then? What do you do when you've come face to face with the bad apple?

That's a lot trickier, right?

There is one clear cut first step for dealing with an unruly parent: Get the coaches, referee or a league official involved immediately. If you take matters into your own hands as a parent, you're just going to exacerbate the problem. Let the people who have some actual type of authority handle it. If nothing else they can issue an ultimatum to the problem-parent like, *"Keep quiet or take your kid home,"* or, *"Keep quiet or your team will forfeit the game."* That usually solves the problem pretty quickly.

Sideline issues are much easier to prevent than to cure, which is why we must do whatever we can to *prevent* the problems. Here are some suggestions for prevention:

- Establish your team / league standards before the season begins. Many leagues now have a Code of Conduct for parents. Some have contracts that parents must sign before their child is allowed to participate. If your league doesn't have standards, push them to get some. Discuss what qualifies as acceptable and unacceptable behavior and make sure everyone gets the memo.

- Your coach should have a meeting at the very beginning of the season, well before the first game, that outlines his goals and his philosophy and what is expected of the parents.

- Have a video camera pointed at the sidelines and make sure everyone knows it's there. Everyone is on his best behavior when he knows he's being filmed.

- One concept that is gaining traction in youth leagues around the country is Silent Sundays, where parents and coaches are asked to refrain from saying anything from the sidelines that can be heard by the players, and to minimize their celebrations after a goal. Silent Sundays have been met with glowing reviews by players, coaches and yes, even parents. They serve as a wonderful reminder that the game belongs to the kids.

- One league I know of used the players to take a proactive approach. Immediately before each game, each player was given a small card. The players ran across the field and handed the cards to their parents. On each card was a list of reminders like:

We play to have fun

Please don't coach from the sidelines

Please don't yell at players, coaches or officials

We aren't professionals so forgive our mistakes

This is our game, not yours

- Encourage your league to reward good behavior. At the end-of-year function, recognize the team whose parents did the best job of setting a great example. Let all the players see that being a good role model doesn't go unnoticed.

Isn't it frightening that we have to actively look for creative solutions to the problems parents cause at soccer games being played by kids? Isn't that just the most bizarre thing? We actually have to protect kids from their own parents during recreational activities? Take a second to let that sink in. If someone from another planet ever lands here and learns of this, we'll be the laughing stock of the galaxy.

Look, more than anything else, your kid wants you to know that he's playing soccer because it's fun. Try to remember that and let it guide you.

55

The Movie In My Head

It's half-time of a U-10 girls' game. Throughout the first half a loudmouth parent has been shouting at the players, the coaches and the refs. He's been turning this game into a miserable experience for everyone. This guy is big and strong and a little bit crazy, so no one is in a hurry to be the one who confronts him.

Across the field, the players are huddled with their coaches. One girl, the man's daughter, walks slowly across the field. A hush overtakes the field. There's nothing but silence. No one is sure what is happening. *Did she quit the team? Did the coach send her home?* She makes the long walk with all eyes upon her. Silence.

She stands face to face with her father. Neither says a word. The father lowers his brow, a not-so-subtle reminder that it would be unwise for her to challenge him. The girl takes a deep breath of courage, reaches into her back pocket, then issues her father a yellow card.

Another second of silence that seems an eternity. Then all at once, the other parents cheer. All of them. The girl turns around and walks back across the field. The man sits there in dumbstruck silence, trying to figure out exactly how he let himself get ambushed. As the applause dies away, he sees the stares of every parent and every player cast upon him. He sees the other players hugging his daughter who is visibly shaken. Realizing he's been beaten, he packs up his chair and walks off toward the parking lot to lick his wounds.

Yeah, it's just my imagination, but don't think it can't happen, especially after people start reading this book. Don't be that dad. Don't star in my movie.

Soccer, above all else, should be fun. Do you want to know why? Because it lacks structure. It lacks the structure of football or baseball where there's a break after every play and where the players have to line up in very specific spots and the coach is telling everyone where to go at any given moment. In soccer, players can run around wherever they want, whenever they want; and aren't kids exceptional at doing exactly that? By its very design, soccer is the perfect game for kids because it lets them be who they are. So you have to wonder how adults manage to screw it all up.

Sometimes I think the answer is as simple as asking ourselves how we would act if our kids were playing a game of backyard Wiffle Ball. We shouldn't behave differently just because a sport is *organized*. We can't let the pageantry of shiny uniforms get the better of us. We've got to be better than that. We've got to hold ourselves to a higher standard. 75% of the kids who've ever started playing soccer should have taught us that by now.

You've done something noble by reading this book. You decided to explore these pages because there was a chance that doing so was in your child's best interest. I applaud you for that! I applaud you because you're going to make soccer a better game for your own kid, and if her team ever plays Izzy's team, you're going to make that experience better for my kid too. So I'd like to say thank you in advance. When your child reaches the end of her playing journey, I hope that you can both look back and see the footprints of the happy feet she has left behind.

I urge you to go forth as a GOLD STAR SOCCER PARENT. I beg of you to remember what you've read here, and to spread the gospel with conviction. Ask your coach or your league to encourage all the parents to read this book in the interest of HAPPY FEET all across this country. Each one of us can help make youth soccer a better experience for everyone.

A FINAL WORD

Thank you for reading my book. I hope you enjoyed it, learned something, laughed a little and feel like you got more than your money's worth. If you did, I hope you will be kind enough to leave me a five-star review on Amazon. Those reviews are an author's currency and it will only take you about 30 seconds.

I also hope this book warrants your recommendation to friends, family and coaches. On behalf of soccer-playing children everywhere, I tried to write something that would become the definitive handbook for soccer parents. If you feel I've done that, I hope you will encourage others to read it also.

If you are interested in buying HAPPY FEET in bulk – at a discounted rate – for your team, club or league, please shoot me an email at coach@soccerpoet.com.

As I was writing this book, I realized that a lot of great people came into my life as coaches. I was very lucky that each one of them furthered my love for soccer and baseball, which eventually landed me a pretty cool career. So I think it's about high time I say thank you to Ed Murzda, Mr. Kraft, Mrs. Costaldo, Bob Seafelt, Bill Berrish, Frank Klein, Dave Paul, Paul Russell, Bill McCafferty, Hank Barber, Dave Potter, Jesse Coleman, Pat Kahny, Bill McQuade, Bill Stout, Santo Rizzo, Bobby Smith, Steve Richards, Jose Gallegos, Jim Regan, Paul Hayward, Graham Ramsey, John Cunningham and Dad.

I was also blessed with two amazing soccer parents who, for eight years, spent one weekend after another shuttling my teammates and I all over the eastern seaboard for soccer tournaments. They also made the six-hour drive out to a great many of my college soccer games and thus earned the nickname of the *Griswolds*. In all that time, I never left a soccer field not looking forward to the next game. I can only hope that every player gets that same joy from his or her soccer career.

A special thank you goes out to Jennifer Barr, Andrew Brower, Kate Burkholder, Dido, Dave Gregson, Ryan Higginbotham, Steve Holeman, Nicole Johnston, Mark MacKain, Catherine Lesnik Marshall, Malcolm Lawrence, Rachael Lehner, Rob Marino, Dom Martelli, Rob Miller, Steve Nugent, Rocky Orezzoli, Scott Paul, George Sasvari, Michael Sabatelle, Roby Stahl and Henry Zapata for their excellent contributions, and to the many coaches who have asked to remain anonymous.

Thank you to Bruce Brown for his fantastic contributions and a lifetime spent advocating for kids. I encourage you to visit his website at www.proactivecoaching.info.

Thank you to Paul 'Neat' Denfeld who quickly graduated from proofreader to editor. I am grateful for his guidance, wisdom and a bevy of excellent suggestions!

Thank you to Dr. Jay Martin for naming *Soccer iQ* as a Top 5 Book of the Year.

Thank you to Ray Alley and Griff Thompson of Southern Soccer Scene for their generous praise and promotion of *Soccer iQ*!

I'm pretty sure that coaches everywhere would like to thank Brian Gotta for his Anonymous Letter from a Volunteer Coach, and I would like to thank him for allowing me to include it in this text. Brian is President of CoachDeck LLC. You can visit his website at www.coachdeck.com. Be sure to sign up for his free newsletter.

I count the voice of the Georgia Bulldogs, the most talented broadcaster in college soccer, Kevin Copp, as a treasured friend and an invaluable ally in the creation of this project. The SoccerPepper™ videos are among KC's many contributions to my life and I shudder to think how much more time it would have taken me to produce a truly inferior product if not for his expertise.

Thank you to the wonderfully talented Aaron Usiskin for rescuing the book's front cover!

Thank you to my awesome wife, Beth, who spent a lot of hours putting this book together.

Thank you to all those soccer-playing kids who never knew that their opinions were being sought for this book.

Thank you to all those soccer parents who dutifully shuffle their children around from one field to the next. You are the ones who keep the soccer world spinning! I hope your soccer experience is joyful and memorable, and that you remember some of the lessons contained in these pages.

And finally, thank you to the youth coaches of America, especially the volunteers!

I hope you'll visit my blog at www.soccerpoet.com and that you'll be my Twitter friend @SoccerPoet. If you have thoughts about this book that you would like to share with me, please email me at coach@soccerpoet.com. I do my best to respond directly to each email.

And I'd like to officially apologize to Andy Reid. You're a great coach and we were lucky to have you as a Philadelphia Eagle.

OTHER BOOKS BY DAN BLANK

Soccer iQ - An Amazon #1 bestseller and named a Top 5 Book of the Year by the *NSCAA Soccer Journal*! The only book written specifically for soccer players. It details the most common mistakes that players make and provides the better solutions. If your soccer player is at least 13-years-old and has a genuine interest in improving, this really is an excellent book. A few pages from now you can read a sample chapter from this title.

Soccer iQ Volume II - Since *Soccer iQ* debuted, many coaches have provided suggestions for an awesome second volume, and this is it. Available 2014.

Rookie - Surviving Your Freshman Year of College Soccer - If you're planning to play college soccer, do yourself a favor and read this. I'm trying to help you. It will be the best money you've ever spent. Available soon.

Everything Your Coach Never Told You Because You're a Girl — Learn what coaches haven't been telling you because you aren't a boy. Available 2014.

OTHER RECOMMENDED
READING / VIEWING

Crashing the Net by Mary Turco – The remarkable story of the United States' first women's Olympic hockey team and their run to the gold medal in Nagano.

Endurance by Alfred Lansing – Every now and then I like to read a survival story because those stories remind me of how good I actually have it and how much adversity the human spirit is capable of overcoming. They also remind me not to whine, which is why I also recommend them to my players, and why you should recommend it to your kids too. *Endurance* recounts Ernest Shackleton's incredible voyage to the South Pole. It is one of the best survival books I have found.

Expectations Lose to the Reality of Sports Scholarships by Bill Pennington – This article appeared in the New York Times in March of 2008 and is a must-read if you have visions of a college soccer scholarship.

Finding the Right Fit – The Naked Truth of the Women's College Soccer Recruiting Process by India Trotter – As someone who has been on both sides of this slippery coin, India speaks plainly about the recruiting process and gives readers a lot of very sound advice. This book is an excellent resource that you need to read before you begin looking at schools.

Girls of Summer by Jere Longman – A behind-the-scenes look at Team USA's 1999 Women's World Cup championship. Includes an eye-opening account of the rise of women's soccer in the U.S. and a fascinating look at the history of the U.S. Women's National Team.

Redefining the Term 'Athlete' — Using the Five Core Values by Bruce Brown (DVD) — One of the great advocates for young athletes defines for the viewer the difference between a *player* and an *athlete*. This DVD is intended for coaches, but parents will also find it insightful.

The Man Watching by Tim Crothers — A biography of Anson Dorrance and an inside look at how he built UNC soccer into an empire. This is one of my all-time favorite books of any genre.

Unbroken by Laura Hillebrand — For all the reasons I suggested you read *Endurance*, read *Unbroken*. It's as inspiring as it is unbelievable. It is the best book I've ever read.

PRAISE FOR SOCCER iQ

Dan, I just wanted to tell you that I consider myself a student of the game. I have read just about every book remotely pertaining to the game. I am also the Director of Coaching of a medium sized club here in P.A, as well as a college coach. After I read your book (twice), I immediately asked my club president for special permission to buy a copy for all my coaches (39 in all). I have never done that before. That is how highly I think of what you wrote. You were spot on with every single topic. I found myself saying, "I say that all the time," for some, or "What a great way to phrase that." I found myself thinking that this relates to my club team, and to my college team. Thank you for writing your book, I think one of the most important things an experienced coach can do is to pass on his knowledge, not protect it. You have done this, and I will do so in turn by providing a copy of your book to my coaches.

- Seamus Donnelly – Director, Penn Legacy Soccer Club
Head Coach - Penn State Harrisburg

Dan what is the fastest way to get 30 copies of your book? I loved the book and I need my players to read it asap.

- Joe Hunter – Head Men's Coach, San Francisco St. University

Finally someone wrote this book! If every soccer player read Soccer iQ, every coach would be a lot happier.

- Mark Francis – Head Coach, University of Kansas

Dan Blank has just written soccer's first definitive text book.

- Colin Carmichael – Head Coach, Oklahoma State University

Soccer iQ is the answer sheet for a soccer exam. It's amazing how often these topics present themselves during the course of a game and a season.

- Jon Lipsitz – Head Coach, University of Kentucky

This book has immediately become required reading for my team. I'll take 30 copies!
- Steve Nugent – Head Coach, Washington State University

Soccer iQ may be the best practical soccer book I have ever red. There's no fluff. Just nuts and bolts principles that we teach every day in training. It'll solve a lot of your soccer problems.
- Steve Holeman – Head Coach, University of Georgia

I came across your book and cannot thank you enough for writing it.
- Rob Mariani – President, Cornwall Soccer, Eastern NY

I just finished reading Soccer iQ (and will read it again ... and again). It's brilliant! On behalf of my current and future players, thank you for the book and insights into the game.
- Todd Clark – Girls Varsity Coach, Severna Park High School

Great job...I read it in the first 24 hours. Please send me the cost so I can recommend it to my players. Congratulations!
- Roby Stahl – Director, AFC Lightning

A really great read. Each concept is broken down in a very short and understandable way for players and coaches. I coach girls and it's nice to have a book written from that perspective.
- Don Hutchinson – (Amazon review)

Most books give you the fundamentals, this books gives you actual coaching advice, more than the fundamentals it is words from a coach to his players. Great read. I've given this book to a couple of people who love to play the game.
- Liz C – (Amazon review)

Soccer iQ is easy to read and it is packed with value. I bought it for my daughter and she couldn't put it down and neither could I. It identifies common mental errors, their causes, effects and solutions. I would recommend it to any girl planning to play in college.
- NJ DAD – (Amazon review)

I've been coaching for many years both Boys and Girls teams. As a coach I always feel that there is something else I should have pointed out to my players, but lacked the insight and or words to convey it to my players. I feel that Dan has touched on many of the "Soccer Problems" that occur in a game but are never addressed by the coach. In each chapter you will find a common soccer problem addressed and dealt with with insight and humor! Like the other reviews, I too plan on getting this book for each of my assistant coaches and players. Thanks for taking the time to write this book Dan.

- Lisa Wilson — (Amazon review)

I'm a soccer mom and I bought Soccer iQ for my son who is an avid player. He enjoyed it so much that we bought another copy for his coach. In the coach's words, "This book is outstanding!" I believe the coach is going to order copies for all the players on our team. I don't have a soccer background but found this book to be very readable. My son and I both enjoyed the simplistic, direct and engaging writing style and he especially found the material to be very informative. It gave me a much better understanding of many of soccer's subtleties. So in short, a player, coach and mom all loved this book.

- S.B. Pinto — (Amazon review)

I coach a girls u-16 club team and bought this book because another coaching friend recommended it (and it was pretty cheap). All I can say is Wow! I read it in one sitting and have reread it several times since.

- SoccercoachTX — (Amazon review)

CHAPTER 18 – THE SHALLOW END

There are times when you are going to have the ball at your feet and room to run in front of you. And you are going to attack that space with gusto! You'll be in the spotlight. The crowd will stand and cheer and shout your name as you fly down the field with the promise of great things to come. Adrenaline will be surging through your veins! Then you're going to come to a wall of defenders that you can't possibly penetrate – not on the dribble, and not with a pass. You've reached a dead end. Going forward is no longer an option. What are you going to do?

At these moments the average player will get caught up in the excitement and keep plowing forward and hoping for the best. And as sure as the sun rises and sets, she will lose the ball.

Look, you've got to be realistic about what's happening around you. In the heat of the moment when everything is exciting and chaotic, you still have to keep your composure and use common sense. When the light at the end of that tunnel starts shrinking and shrinking, you've got to have the composure and the common sense to put on the brakes and turn around.

It's okay. Trust me. We understand. And we appreciate the fact that you are helping our team keep the ball as opposed to going on your own little glorified suicide mission. *We get it.*

In these moments it would behoove you to remember a lesson you learned at the swimming pool many years ago. Do you remember the first time you were in an in-ground pool, when you were just a kid and still couldn't swim? You slinked into the shallow end because it was safe there. But you wanted to test your boundaries so you would take one step after another toward the deep end. You'd let the water level come right up under your nose. Then you soon reached a spot where the water was over your head and you realized you were in danger. Then what did you do? You kicked and splashed your way back to the shallow end as fast as you possibly could. And that was *a really good* choice!

The same thing goes for soccer. You've got to realize when the water has gotten too deep and when it has, simply step on the ball and swim back toward the shallow end. Help your team keep the ball. You can't win without it.

Note for Coaches: There is not a doubt in my mind that you have players that suffer from this malady. Every team does. Here's my advice: Get it on video and show your team. Then use the swimming pool metaphor because it's memorable and easy to understand. I've literally had players shouting, "SHALLOW END!" to a teammate who was about to dribble herself into trouble. When players are reciting your metaphors, you know they stuck. Now, contradictory to everything you've just read in this chapter, a few times in your life you may coach that very special player who can in fact occasionally dribble her way through that human wall. Don't talk her out of it. Just sit back and enjoy the show while she wins games for you.

ABOUT THE AUTHOR

Dan Blank is the author of the Amazon bestseller, *Soccer iQ*, and has been coaching college soccer for over twenty years. He is the first coach in Southeastern Conference history to lead the conference's best defense in consecutive years at different universities (Ole Miss 2009, Georgia 2010). He has an 'A' License from the USSF and an Advanced National Diploma from the NSCAA. You can buy his books and read his blog at www.soccerpoet.com.

REFRENCES, FOOTNOTES

[1] Source: Youth Sports in America: An Overview by Seefedlt, Ewing and Walk, 1992

[2] Source: Minnesota Amateur Sports Commission, Athletic Footwear Association, USA Today Survey, Michigan State

[3] Source: Overview of Youth Sports Programs in the United States; Institute for the Study of Youth Sports; Michigan State University.

22485977R00114

Printed in Poland
by Amazon Fulfillment
Poland Sp. z o.o., Wrocław